ELEMENTS OF ETIQUETTE

ELEMENTS OF ETIQUETTE

A Guide
to
Table Manners
in an
Imperfect
World

CRAIG CLAIBORNE

WILLIAM MORROW AND COMPANY, INC.
NEW YORK

It is the policy of William Morrow and Company, Inc., and its imprints and affiliates, recognizing the importance of preserving what has been written, to print the books we publish on acid-free paper, and we exert our best efforts to that end..

Library of Congress Cataloging-in-Publication Data
Claiborne, Craig.
Elements of etiquette : a guide to table manners in an imperfect world / Craig Claiborne.
p.   cm.
ISBN 0-688-07402-2
1. Table etiquette. I. Title.
BJ2041.C53   1992   CIP
395'.54–dc20   92-7954
Printed in the United States
First Edition
1 2 3 4 5 6 7 8 9 10

Produced by Smallwood & Stewart, Inc., New York
Edited by Laurie Orseck
Designed and Illustrated by Michelle Wiener

For Yanou Collart, with love and gratitude

ACKNOWLEDGMENTS

There are many people to whom I owe a serious debt of gratitude for this book. They number my severest critics when I have been seated at the table, including my mother, Kathleen Craig Claiborne; Monsieur Conrad Tuor, who was master of my training for table service at the Hotel School of the Swiss Hotel Keepers Association in Lausanne, Switzerland, almost forty years ago; Le Pavillon's Henri Soulé, America's ultimate restaurant keeper; Eric Kuhn, a young newspaperman from my hometown of East Hampton, New York, who browsed through and criticized my manuscript in its very early stages; Ann Bramson, a good friend and my editor at William Morrow, who had faith and believed in what I have produced here; and, finally, Ella Stewart and John Smallwood of Smallwood and Stewart, who with supercritical eye and good taste brought this book to its conclusion. It was they who added innumerable good things as related to style and presentation.

CONTENTS

INTRODUCTION

One of the lamentable casualties of the recent social revolution is the daily practice of etiquette. It is not that we no longer live in a world in which every dinner is formal and men are left to smoke their cigars after the meal. I do not long for the severe and pompous dictates of earlier generations; we are all relieved to be spared the stuffy exchanges that typified social events of that earlier age. I refer, instead, to a society that places no value on manners, a society that seems to believe that manners have no place in the order of things.

It is small wonder that people of the present generation do not know what is expected of them. In fact, for the multitudes in the age of greed, punk music, and the ME generation, nothing is expected. In our changing environment, confusion reigns, and there is no longer a widely accepted standard for public behavior. Nowhere is this loss more acutely felt than at table, for it is here that insecurity, insincerity, and insubordination rule.

Good manners, like good taste, derive from

sensibility and simple common sense. Once mastered, that concept can be abiding and guiding. For example, it is polite to answer invitations promptly, not to wait to see if something more to your preference comes up. Similarly, it is polite to arrive on time; today's host must be understandably tolerant, for guests routinely arrive forty-five minutes or even an hour late. (I am amazed that more home kitchens do not have commercial steam tables to accommodate such unfortunate behavior.) And the picky, plodding eater should not expect her fellow diners to wait for her to clean her plate before moving on to the next course.

The aim of entertaining is to share good will; the practice of etiquette is the means by which this is accomplished. Hosts or hostesses, of course, are not without their own responsibilities. At a dinner, the hostess acts as guide, and her guests defer to her lead. She will bear in mind that the dinner table is not an appropriate setting for conversations of an intimate nature, be it romance or health, nor should such depressing topics as financial problems, career dilemmas, and family crises be examined. And silverware should be the heavy metal at a dinner party, not the music.

Here, then, in *Elements of Etiquette* is what I consider a sensible guide to good manners. It is based on my lifetime of experiences as a guest and a host. It does not present a litany of rigid strictures for the reader's adherence, nor does it dwell on such obscure occasions as the ultra-formal, seventeen-course dinner. Rather, it is intended for the guest and host alike who wish to act with confidence and grace in any type of dining situation. It is written for the countless thousands who look forward to memorable meals, served up with camaraderie and easy laughter . . . for it is their laughter and fellowship that make certain evenings linger in the memory.

CHAPTER ONE

THE BEST-LAID PLANS

Nothing is more hopeless

than a scheme of merriment.

SAMUEL JOHNSON

To my mind, entertaining well is the epitome of hospitality. Not everyone, however, shares my passion. There seem to be two types of hosts and hostesses ~ those who relish every moment of a social occasion, and those who dread even the most informal gathering. What is it that thrills some and strikes terror in the hearts of others? I think it is simply that successful hosts know what is expected of them and are not intimidated by the fear of doing the wrong thing. It is inevitable that these hosts approach a meal with interest and enthusiasm. The result of this attitude is that everyone involved is able to have a good time. After all, sharing a meal is one of life's great pleasures ~ it should be fun.

Planning and foresight are a host's strongest allies. Some well-thought-out questions early on will reap great rewards later: Will there be enough seating? Will guests be able to eat their food comfortably? Is an elaborate menu feasible? Should it be a sit-down dinner, or is a buffet more appropriate?

Formal sit-down dinners are elegant, but important events can be just as wonderfully celebrated with an imaginative and stylish buffet. One of the most agreeable parties I ever attended was an engagement party held on the beach at East Hampton. Whatever style you decide upon, do not overreach. The point of the occasion is for everyone to enjoy himself. Being a harried cook, waiter, and host all in one will not do much to put your guests at ease.

Do a head count and chair count beforehand to be sure you have sufficient seating for everyone. You do not want to have seventy-five foot-weary guests trying to steal each other's chairs at your overcrowded cocktail party, nor do you want frazzled guests juggling awkward plates of food because you forgot that even at a buffet seating is required.

SERVICE WITH A STYLE

There are many different styles of food service, one of which should be right for your needs. Basically, here is what you can choose from:

Buffet: Guests serve themselves and seat themselves. Food is arranged on platters placed on a table or sideboard. Stacks of plates and flatware are also on the table.

Family-style: A casual, informal gathering where guests are seated at a table. Place cards may be used if desired. Courses are placed on the table or sideboard where they remain during the entire meal. Guests generally serve themselves.

Formal: A seated dinner usually for six or more. Dinner consisting of five or more courses is served by waiters from serving trays. No serving dishes are ever left on the table.

He that hath more manners

than he ought,

Is more a fool than he

thought.

THOMAS D'URFEY

To get into the best society

nowadays, one has either to

feed people, amuse people, or

shock people.

OSCAR WILDE

If you are considering a formal dinner, remember that while it is the height of sophistication, it is also the height of showmanship and organization. A formal dinner is, by its nature, designed to spare your guests from any contact with serving trays or food platters. Usually, sometime after cocktails are served, dinner is announced and guests enter a dining area and are seated at a table that is already set with fine crystal, china, candles, and flowers. All food is presented individually to each guest from trays held by a server. While there is no reason a host or hostess could not capably do this on his or her own, I would recommend that for any guest list over eight, you consider hiring outside help. In addition, a formal dinner usually requires large amounts of dinnerware, silverware, stemware, and linens. The cleanup after this sort of formality is always enormous.

THE SEATED BUFFET

A lively and expeditious way to entertain a large number of guests is at a seated buffet. If you have a good-natured mix of guests, there will be a feeling of festivity in the air. Food is arranged on platters and is presented on a table, sideboard, kitchen island ~ anywhere there is room for guests to help themselves. If your guest list is large, two separate areas of dinnerware, silverware, napkins, and glasses can be set up; for a more elegant buffet, place settings should already be at tables. Presliced meat makes for easy handling and eating. It is always bothersome to have to carve one's own food at a buffet table, and hacked-up meat carcasses are unsightly. Appealing arrangements of foods that can be eaten together harmoniously can be offered all at once. If you are serving foods intended to be eaten course by course, only one course should be placed on the table at a time. This is demanding to do if you alone are serving, and you may want to enlist the services of your spouse or a friend to help with dish removal.

Good manners are made up

of petty sacrifices.

RALPH WALDO EMERSON

MENU PLANNING

While most of this subject falls in the category of "entertaining" rather than "etiquette," several considerations will go a long way in making both host and guest comfortable and adept at at table. Many anxious hosts create overly elaborate menus that distract and confuse their guests. A more considerate approach is to center a menu on those foods that are fresh, simple to prepare, and above all, easy to eat.

Many hosts enjoy basing their dinner parties on a theme and carrying this theme through to the menu. Be certain to inform your guests of your intentions when you issue your invitations.

Halloween parties, for example, are usually raucous, casual affairs, and a guest would be rightfully annoyed if he arrived dressed as Fred Flintstone and was expected to sit through a five-course sit-down meal. If you plan a buffet featuring a theme, a nice touch is to place a handwritten menu on the buffet table or sideboard. That way your guests will know what to expect and can pace themselves accordingly. You certainly don't want your guests leaving your party in search of the nearest pizza parlor because they assumed there would be another course after the Maryland crab cakes. On the other hand, a considerate host does not overdo a menu, forcing guests to load up on rich or cholesterol-laden foods. Most people today are well aware of the trend toward lighter foods, and while hosts might like to offer their guests a "treat" of something rich and special, usually they will balance this with a selection of other nonthreatening dishes. Few people over the age of ten actually benefit from fatty foods, and in today's health-conscious climate most guests appreciate a meal that does not require a cardiologist in attendance.

De gustibus non disputandum est. (There is no disputing about taste.)

LATIN PROVERB

WHOSE DIET IS IT ANYWAY?

Menu planning brings up another rather serious subject. You are invited to dinner at a new friend's home for the first time and are faced with a quandary: Not only are you a vegetarian, but your husband is allergic to all cheeses. Should you share this information with your hostess beforehand, or should you take your chances with her menu? As a host and a person who loves to cook, I would emphatically recommend a course of honesty. It is truly discourteous to allow your host to go to the trouble of preparing foods that have every chance of not being eaten. It is far better, and not at all offensive, to accept the invitation by saying, "Of course we would love to come, but please let me tell you about our special food situation, so that you can decide if we will fit in with your plans." A host who knows in advance can, with grace and skill, adjust the menu to fit everyone's needs.

Of course the music is a great difficulty. You see, if one plays good music, people don't listen, and if one plays bad music, people don't talk.

OSCAR WILDE

THE SOUND OF MUSIC

There is no right or wrong decision about having background music at your dinner party. Dining is an exceedingly sensory pleasure, so it is important to calculate the effect that music will create. Some hosts always choose soothing background music, while others regard a room reverberating with lively conversation to be the sweeter sound. It really is a question of personal taste. It is wise to consider your guests' preferences as well as your own ~ perhaps you love that album of show tunes, but if it is not a guaranteed hit, it might best be saved for a spirited clean-up time. I know serious music critics who denounce the use of music of the masters ~ Bach and Beethoven, for example ~ as an accompaniment for food. They look upon it as a desecration of the arts. On the positive side, background music can sometimes bridge awkward silences, itself becoming a conversation point if nothing else. Low, gentle classical music is a judicious choice as far as I am concerned; I find loud rock odious unless you are serving hot dogs and hamburgers al fresco. Whatever your choice, please keep the sound at a civilized level so that a chance for conversation still exists.

HIRED HANDS

The most delicious pleasure is

to cause that of other people.

LA BRUYERE

When you are hosting a large dinner party or buffet, expert outside help may be more than a luxury ~ it can be a sanity saver. Should your budget allow this, the addition of a bartender, waiter, or waitress can free you to spend more time with your guests. If you have no experience supervising or hiring help, ask for a recommendation from a friend or acquaintance whose opinion you trust. Furthermore, if you have never hosted the type of party you are considering, do not be embarrassed to have a run-through with the people you have hired. Clarity is the greatest favor you can bestow here. Be specific about what you expect beforehand; this will go far to reduce confusion later. Discuss the time of arrival, departure, clean-up duties, hourly wage, and style of dress or uniform. And do resist the temptation to put on the dog; it would be preposterous to have a waiter in black tie serving corn on the cob at your Fourth of July picnic. If you are especially pleased with an employee's performance, a gratuity is always appropriate.

I consider it good manners to introduce the server or servers to all family members and, in particular, to the guest of honor if there is to be one. The guest of honor must at least be pointed out, as he or she would naturally be served first. And do remember that whoever you are hiring is a human being, too. Do not suddenly act like the lord or lady of the manor and treat this person like a servant. Such behavior will only make you look like an amateur.

Manners have been somewhat cynically defined to be a contrivance of wise men to keep fools at a distance.

RALPH WALDO EMERSON

The guest list

Making up a guest list is where the host combines the skills of a diplomat, chemist, and prophet, sowing the seeds of disaster or success. The goal is clear: to put together those personality combinations that can spark off each other, at the same time being careful not to inadvertently create any combustible mixtures. Now is the time to scan through your memory bank to select those guests who inspire harmony, not discord.

I have always found a large buffet, as well as the much-maligned cocktail party, to be wonderful vehicles for absorbing a broad range of personalities and ages. Guests are usually not forced upon one another, at least not for long, and that can make for a lively scene.

THE INVITATION

[Society is] a bore. But to be

out of it is simply a tragedy.

OSCAR WILDE

Gone are the days when social invitations were hand-delivered by one's servant. Not only are invitations issued by mail and messenger, but more and more by telephone and those debatable miracles of technology, the answering machine and the facsimile machine. Whatever form invitations assume, one idea above all must prevail, and that is that the invitations be gracious and sincere.

I find nothing more impeccable or flattering than the handwritten invitation ~ far more appealing than something engraved, expensive, or stiffly worded. Depending on the occasion, your invitations can range from the traditional to the more lighthearted. For instance, an invitation to an informal dinner party for a good friend's new novel could carry the message:

Please join us to celebrate Kenneth Writer's new book, *Big Advance*, on Friday, the thirteenth of March, at eight o'clock, 971 Greene Street, New York City

You may include the word "Informal" in the lower left-hand corner along with R.S.V.P. and your telephone number should you want telephone replies. If the occasion is very informal, you can certainly send store-bought invitations. While these do not have the same cachet as a handwritten invitation, they are commonly used and perfectly acceptable.

When staging a very large party, such as an open house, some hosts cut down on potential paperwork by writing "Regrets Only" under the R.S.V.P. line. Unless the recipient declines, the host will assume his invitation has been accepted.

Invitations to highly formal sit-down dinners are usually written to a time-honored social formula. Many people feel self-conscious using this form, but should the occasion dictate, the following, written on light-colored, heavy notepaper, would be perfect invitation etiquette:

Mr. August Fowler requests the pleasure of your company [or you may add names here] at dinner on Friday, the eighth of November, at eight o'clock, 827 Greene Street, New York City

The ornament of a house is the friends who frequent it.

RALPH WALDO EMERSON

I have often seen men prove

unmannerly by too much

manners and importune by

too much courtesy.

MONTAIGNE

If you are going to the effort of handwriting your invitations, it is a good idea to keep your message legible. Extravagant calligraphy may be your hobby, but unless your guests know the time and day to arrive, your party may not be as successful as you hope. Common sense dictates that you clearly write the date, time, place, and whether an R.S.V.P. is expected. And please, do not force your guests to play twenty questions trying to figure out what the occasion is. Indicate "Dinner in honor of my niece, Miss Constance Virtue," or "Cocktails at 7:30. Dinner at 8:00."

All invitations should be sent out so there is enough time to receive responses. Two weeks is a general rule for written and telephone invitations to informal dinners, certainly less time if the occasion is a more spontaneous, last-minute gathering. For very formal affairs requiring great expenditures of money, time, and planning, invitations are mailed four to six weeks before the occasion. It is considered presumptuous to add a date by which the invitee must respond.

As we shall see, guests are expected to reply quickly, but if they fail to do so, a host may feel perfectly free to send out a reminder card, or place a reminder telephone call.

THE RESPONSE

In any discussion of etiquette, it seems that a great deal of emphasis is placed on the obligations of the host or hostess. Undoubtedly, in most entertaining situations, the host does bear much of the responsibility for ensuring that his guests have a good time. But not all. I feel it is important to point out that guests, too, have obligations to the host, and foremost among those are acting courteously, being sensitive, and entering into the spirit of the occasion with perceptible good will. Do not feel obligated to accept an invitation if it is an occasion you truly dread. And do not accept an invitation if there is any chance that you might cast a pall on your host's hard work. If, for example, you have just been passed over for a promotion, do not look upon an invitation as an opportunity for group sympathy; a social gathering is the time to make other guests glad to be in your company.

The interaction between guest and host begins with the invitation. The ball is in the guest's court once the invitation has been received. It is, by the nature of his reply, that the guest will exhibit his politeness. I believe there can be no more proper or courteous a reply than a speedy one ~ especially if it is in the affirmative. If you must decline, procrastination will not endear you to your busy hostess. Since most of us take turns at being either guests or hosts, we know how vexing it is to put together a dinner party and have to chase down dilatory repliers.

As to how to reply, you will always be on safe ground if your response parallels the style of the invitation. Of course, this does not mean that if your invitation arrived in a pot of freesia, so should your response. It means, rather, that telephone invitations can be followed by telephone replies, formal invitations with handwritten notes. As for leaving acceptances on an answering machine, my inclination is to express my intentions to my host directly ~ though I must defer to the usefulness of these machines since busy people are often difficult to reach. A guest has the choice of writing a reply even to a telephone invitation; it is always a generous expression of delight in being invited. A short note stating that you "look forward with pleasure to the dinner on Saturday, March 13th" is all that is required.

Formal invitations demand a timely, written reply if the R.S.V.P. is not followed by a telephone number. Again, a short note, handwritten on a neutral-colored card, is proper:

> Mr. and Mrs. Charles Bovary accept
> with pleasure the kind invitation of
> Mrs. Sigerson-Morrison for Saturday, the
> thirteenth of June, at eight o'clock,
> New York City

[Etiquette is] simply to cherish such a habitual respect for mankind as may prevent us from disgusting our fellow-creatures for the sake of a present indulgence.

MARY WOLLSTONECRAFT

Or:

Miss Maybel Evans regrets she cannot
accept Mr. James Blandings's kind invitation
for Tuesday, the seventh of September,
New York City

A reply to an informal invitation may be
written in a more casual fashion, on personal
notepaper, a postcard, or whatever you have that
is charming and lighthearted. An acceptance
need only say, "I accept with pleasure," or "We
are so looking forward to it!" A regret may say,
"I'm so sorry to miss your party. We'll be in
Scotland for the salmon run."

Should you be invited as a couple, and one of
you is unable to attend, courtesy demands that
you both decline the invitation to allow your
hostess the option of inviting another couple. Of
course, if the hostess urges you to attend anyway,
it is perfectly acceptable to do so.

And in all cases when you must decline an
invitation, spare your host any long, tedious explanations. A simple "I'm very sorry, but we
can't make it" is sufficient. You must never imply
that the party cannot possibly survive without
your attendance, which is unfortunately what
many overly devastated replies suggest.

Confidence does more to

make conversation than wit.

LA ROCHEFOUCAULD

CALLING IT OFF

The costliness of keeping

friends does not lie in what

one does for them, but in

what one, out of consideration

for them, refrains from doing.

HENRIK IBSEN

Occasionally, one is in the regrettable position of being forced to cancel an acceptance at the last minute. Illness or family misfortune are valid reasons ~ certainly never the caddish excuse that "something else has come up." Resist the temptation to put off a difficult conversation and notify your hostess immediately. Explain simply and sincerely why you are unable to attend. Sending flowers along with a note would be a generous added gesture.

By the way, an acceptance for a dinner party means staying for the entire meal, from cocktails to coffee. For some reason, there has been a lamentable growth in the practice of guests springing to their feet after one or two courses, blowing kisses to their host, and dashing off to their next engagement. This behavior is unforgivable, no matter how overburdened by social obligations one may be. If a guest knows she cannot stay for the entire meal, she must notify her host in advance ~ and this does not mean as she is walking through the door. It is only at the insistence of the host that such a guest should even consider putting in her brief appearance.

MUSICAL CHAIRS

It seems self-evident: Every guest at a party should have a comfortable seat. It is not. I have attended too many dinners where this simple, basic notion is overlooked. So for the sake of anyone planning a party, let me declare the absolute necessity of providing guests with chairs. This is just as true for a buffet for forty as a cozy dinner for six. It is simply bad manners to assume that your guests would enjoy perching on sofa armrests or, worse yet, standing up during a buffet meal. If you do not have enough chairs, and cannot borrow what you need, consider renting them ~ or trimming your guest list.

Guests with special conditions must be given seating that is appropriate. You do not want a gout-stricken relative struggling in and out of a bean-bag chair during cocktails, nor would you wish to offer a delicate Louis Quinze side chair to a guest whose girth resembles that of a sumo wrestler. But bear in mind here that hosts do walk a fine line between being considerate and being too deferential. Make your guests feel comfortable without appearing overly solicitous. Be careful not to give anyone the feeling that he has been parked in the "Handicapped Only" zone.

It is almost a definition of a gentleman to say he is one who never inflicts pain.

JOHN HENRY

CARDINAL NEWMAN

SEATING PLANS

Now comes the part that requires artistry ~ creating a seating plan. Your objective is to pair guests in ways that will bring out the best in each. If you are hosting a buffet, a seating plan is unnecessary, but formal or sit-down dinners can be immeasurably enhanced by one. For one thing, most guests appreciate not being forced to make seating decisions by themselves. For another, it affords the host more control of conversational possibilities.

Traditionally at seated dinners, the arrangement is to alternate men and women, although at informal meals this "rule" may be relaxed. Most hosts believe in separating husbands and wives for fear that they will visibly bore each other. I think it is courteous to place guests near those whose company they would most enjoy ~ and if that is a spouse, more power to the couple. In general, however, try placing quieter types next to the more extroverted so they may balance and play off each other. It is best to avoid obvious mismatches, such as a guest who is hard of hearing next to a friend who cannot seem to talk above a whisper.

Guests of honor are to be accorded the seat that commands the most elegant or interesting view of the dining room. This seat may face a garden, for example, or an especially inviting part of the room.

[Etiquette is] the courtly manners of any two-legged predatory animal.

ELBERT HUBBARD

PLACE CARDS

Depending on my mood, I either tell close friends outright where to sit or let them select their own seating. For hosts with exceptionally strong convictions about seating arrangements, or for very large dinner parties, place cards can guide guests to the places at table where they will sit and, hopefully, find congenial souls next to them. Using a heavy, fine-quality paper stock, hand-letter each guest's name in a pleasing color ink. Be sure the names are spelled correctly and are easy to read. First names only are appropriate for an informal dinner, or for close friends; duplicate Johns or Beths can be identified by their initials. If there are any titled guests present with whom one is not on a first-name basis, their title should be included as well.

Center the place cards behind each place setting. They should be removed as soon as everyone is seated. If the cards are made for a special occasion, or are written in a beautiful calligraphic hand, guests may certainly take them home at the end of the evening. Under no circumstances, however, does an adult worthy of the title shuffle place cards around to suit his own seating desires.

[Manners are] your station

in life.

EUGENE F. BRUSSEL

CHAPTER TWO

The perfect host, the perfect guest

Doing a good job as host or guest takes effort. By knowing in advance what is expected, we can sail happily through any social situation. If luck is the residue of design, then for every host and guest, the sweet taste of success comes from hard work and attention to detail. Ignorance about simple etiquette should never interfere with the pleasures that lie ahead.

DRESSING FOR DINNER

There are still rules pertaining to proper attire that, if followed, can go a long way toward making everyone feel comfortable and worry-free. First of all, if you are attending a formal dinner, plan to dress formally. For men this can mean anything from a dark business suit and tie to a tuxedo or dinner jacket. Men cannot go far wrong in a conservatively tailored wool suit that is either black or dark navy blue. Women, on the other hand, are blessed with greater fashion latitude. A short-skirted dinner dress or evening slacks of satin or velvet are just as appropriate as a gown at a sit-down dinner.

A man dressed in a tuxedo for a formal affair who then must go to an informal meal in either a private home or restaurant is better off going home to change into street clothes. If time does not permit, it is perfectly permissible to wear the

You can't get high aesthetic tastes, like trousers, ready made.

W. S. GILBERT

tuxedo to the ensuing engagement, although a brief explanation should be offered. The black tie and tuxedo jacket, however, should not be removed: To do so would give the appearance of someone ready to retire for the evening.

At a buffet or family-style dinner one should take one's cue from the time of day the event is to be held. For women, a pants outfit or even a sporty dress would be fine at any time of day. For men, a classic navy blazer and gray wool slacks are always appropriate, as is a conservative sports jacket. At a brunch, dress can be taken much more casually, especially in the country, where blue jeans and linen are much more prevalent. Men can always remove their jackets, and perhaps their ties, if the occasion is informal enough, but I think it shows respect to come dressed to one's highest standards. I consider "underdressed" to be the greater social crime.

In any event, it is the host's obligation to communicate in some way just what level of dress is expected. Written invitations should specify. Telephone invitations allow uncertain guests to ask. It is the sensitive host who will impart this information clearly and straightforwardly; playing games by saying, "Oh, just anything will do," does everyone a disservice.

It is not difficult to be unconventional in the eyes of the world when your unconventionality is but the convention of your set.

W. SOMERSET MAUGHAM

A WHIFF OF FRAGRANCE

The billion-dollar perfume and cologne industry promotes the openhanded use of expensive scents as part of our "lifestyle." Despite this, let it be said here that both men and women wearing fragrances run the risk of being a miserable distraction to their dinner partners and an affront to those who are serious about their food. A discreet touch of perfume or after-shave is wholly acceptable, but it should not be apparent to those sitting near you.

BEARING GIFTS

Civility costs nothing and buys everything.

LADY MARY WORTLEY

MONTAGU

Can a gift from a guest ever be offensive? I would say yes. This issue merits attention if only because guests do unwittingly offend hosts by showing up with the "wrong" present. In certain places no self-respecting guest would arrive for a meal without at least one cardboard box from a favorite bakery. Others feel barbaric without an armor of at least two feet of chrysanthemums. The truth is that a guest never really has to bring anything at all, except for his own good cheer. But if you wish to bring something to express your appreciation in advance, think twice about what the gift may actually imply. If it will in any way create additional work for your hostess, it is

24

a poor idea. Certainly avoid bringing along anything you are transparently trying to "unload," such as that peculiar bottle of wine from Paraguay or the five-pound box of Jordan almonds your aunt sent you. Remember that gifts of food in particular can upset a host's carefully planned menu. Two dozen cannolis may not be appropriate following a meal of frittata. And flowers that require arranging can send your host off on a search for a vase just when he wants to be with his guests. Wouldn't a small pot of flowering bulbs be more considerate? Or a tiny box of imported chocolates?

Of course, you can always send a flower arrangement the day of the party; this is an especially gracious gesture from the guest of honor. Or if you are arriving with armsful of freshly cut hydrangeas from your country garden, a phone call to your hostess beforehand will give her time to locate the perfect Roseville vase.

Must a host serve a bottle of wine or dish brought by a guest? This point of etiquette is perhaps responsible for more discomfort and hurt feelings than any other, so let it be stated definitively: A host is never obligated to serve a gift of food or drink, and a guest is never justified in feeling slighted if his does not appear on the dinner table. It may be served if the host deems it compatible with the menu, and if he feels his other guests will enjoy it. If not, he

If a man does not make new acquaintances as he advances through life, he will soon find himself alone. A man, Sir, should keep his friendships in constant repair.

HENRY ADAMS

should politely thank the guest, telling him how very much he is looking forward to savoring it in the near future. The guest should never insist.

GUESS WHO'S (NOT) COMING TO DINNER

There will always be occasions that test the limits of a host's diplomacy. Dealing with unexpected extra guests is one of them. Regardless of the circumstances under which surprise guests arrive, it is the host who exhibits grace under pressure and acts as though he is delighted with this unforeseen addition who wins my praise. Of course, anyone who puts a host in a situation like this would do well to secure the name of a good florist for a lavish thank-you the next day.

If a man be gracious and

courteous to strangers,

it shows he is a citizen of

the world.

FRANCIS BACON

But are there circumstances under which a guest may ask to bring along a last-minute guest? The answer must be yes. Suppose your cousin arrived in town unexpectedly. She is acquainted with the host and you think she would fit in splendidly with his other guests. If you and the host are close friends, you can certainly bring up this idea. The host obviously has the right to deny the request, but I personally find that an unexpected alteration in my plans usually spices up an evening, and I seem to be able to stretch most meals to include another person.

FASHIONABLY ON TIME

Many people are still wondering when they should arrive at a social function. While the time devoted to such reflections might be better spent thinking of interesting topics to contribute to-ward the evening's success, I would like to say that the time to arrive is the time stated, with a possible ten- to fifteen-minute grace period. No sensitive guest should inconvenience a host by arriving much later, and no sensitive host can sacrifice the comfort of guests who have already arrived for the comfort of those who insist upon being unforgivably late.

Punctuality is the politeness

of kings.

LOUIS XVIII OF FRANCE

GREETINGS

All is ready: The drinks tray is out, the seat-ing comfortable, the lighting soft and relaxing. The doorbell rings ~ your first guests. You open the door . . . and your mind goes totally blank, incapable of remembering their names.

This scenario is a nightmare for any host or hostess. We all have temporary blackouts, but it is the host's obligation to know the details of the guest list, and to review them with family mem-bers. If caught in the regrettable situation of memory loss, one can admit this graciously by stating, "I'm drawing a blank. Sometimes I can't remember my own name; now I've forgotten yours." A poised and considerate guest will realize that this is not a slight directed at her, and will be quick to let the moment pass with grace and good humor.

The tone of the evening starts at the doorway. Now is the time to make each guest feel special and welcome. I prefer to allow my guests to actually pass through the doorway before physically greeting them. This is far more inviting than uncomfortable kisses and handshakes in what might be the cold and rain. The sensitive host should greet each guest in a friendly and effusive way without being presumptuous. In general, women guests may be greeted by the host or hostess with a handclasp and a light kiss on the cheek if the relationship is that affectionate. A male guest may also be greeted with a kiss and handclasp from the hostess, and a handshake from the host. Remember, it is an unbreakable rule of courtesy to shake the hand of anyone who offers it, male or female.

INTRODUCTIONS

It is unfathomable to me why a matter as fundamental as an introduction is so often bungled. To be able to introduce people properly is a mark of refinement. There is nothing arcane about knowing how to do so gracefully. Traditionally, men are presented to women: "Sarah, may I introduce Archer Hamilton? Archer, this is our Latin teacher, Sarah Stewart." (The only exception to the rule of introducing a man to a woman is if the man in question is of very high rank, such as President of the United States, a Supreme Court justice, or the Archbishop of Canterbury, in which case one would be correct to present the woman to the man.)

It is also customary to present younger people to older: "Mother, may I introduce our new neighbor, Emma Davidson? Emma, I'd like you to meet my mother, Mildred Twining."

Today, women generally shake hands upon being introduced to either a man or a woman, and many prefer to rise. (In the past women remained seated during an introduction except when meeting a much older person, in which case it was considered respectful to stand.) While women still have the option of sitting or standing, in these days of greater professional status for women, and with a more heightened awareness of their achievements, I think it is a demonstration of equality for a woman to greet all newcomers on their level.

Children, by the way, should not be exempt from this kind of proper behavior. Whether it is from parental laziness or overindulgence, it is unimaginable to me how children who are al-

True politeness consists in being easy one's self, and in making everyone about one as easy as one can.

ALEXANDER POPE

lowed to be rude and indifferent to adults will ever grow up to be "polite." They must be taught to be respectful, to stand up when a guest enters a room, to shake hands if offered, to speak clearly, and to look at adults when spoken to. Children are always introduced to adults, without resorting to condescending or silly language. A parent may say, "Mrs. Byrnes, I would like you to meet my daughter, Annalee. Annalee, Mrs. Byrnes also has a ten-year-old daughter, Kate." Under no circumstance should a child address an adult by his or her first name unless given permission to do so. Children are also expected to say good-bye, or good-night, to their parents' guests.

At a very large gathering ~ a party, a business meeting, or wherever there is a bewilderment of people, including even casual acquaintances ~ do not presume your host will be able to introduce you to everyone. You should shake hands with individuals and give your name. Forgive their forgetfulness, if there is any, and make it easy on those with a lax memory. There is, of course, such a thing as carrying this too far: If you walk into a room where you are absolutely certain you are known to all those assembled there, do not reintroduce yourself.

[A cocktail party is] an affair where you meet old friends you never met before.

FULTON BRYAN

OF COCKTAILS, COASTERS, AND CANAPES

Be sure your guests are comfortably settled ~ wraps taken, introductions made ~ before offering them cocktails or hors d'oeuvres. If you have prepared only a single type of cocktail such as a pitcher of vodka sours ~ a practice I do not advise ~ and have no other drinks to offer, you should make this clear by saying, "We are pouring vodka sours tonight. May I offer you one?"

Canapés or light appetizers should be kept on the dainty side. Less is more in the philosophy of cocktail snacks. Save those fried mozzarella sticks for your eight-year-old's birthday party or a barbecue.

Of course, drinks should be served with cocktail napkins for the simple reason that hands become uncomfortably chilled when holding an iced beverage. I arrange stacks of extra cocktail napkins and coasters near seating areas so that guests do not have to search desperately for a place to put their drinks. Just as a considerate guest will never rest a cocktail or iced beverage on a book, magazine, or piece of fine wood furniture, a considerate host will always provide coasters. If none is within sight, a guest may ask for one. But never, under any circumstances, should a host pick up a guest's drink and put it on a coaster for him. That would be tantamount

Gossip is vice enjoyed

vicariously.

ELBERT HUBBARD

to reprimanding him for not being sensitive or polite enough to do it himself.

As for the peculiar practice of serving drinks with swizzle sticks in them, please refrain. These tacky bits of plastic only become instant garbage. It takes but one swift movement with a bar spoon to stir a drink. Similarly, soda straws are just as inane. I once took malicious delight in seeing an athletic-looking man in a restaurant holding a glass in one hand with his index and middle finger while tying to keep the soda straw in place. He inadvertently turned his head quickly and poked himself in the eye. Since we do not want guests leaving our parties with seeing-eye dogs, please ~ never use these preposterous objects. If however, you are served a drink with either a swizzle stick or a straw, you are perfectly within your rights to remove it and sip your beverage from the rim of the glass.

JUGGLING ACT

One of the drawbacks of a cocktail party or a buffet-style meal is the need to juggle plates, silver, and glassware all at once. Ideally, each guest has been provided with a comfortable seat and a surface nearby on which to rest dishes while eating or drinking.

Drinks should be served in glasses only half full. This is not because of a lack of generosity, but rather because a lesser amount is easier to

[A cocktail party is] a gathering

at which drinks mix people.

ANONYMOUS

handle in the acrobatic environment of a cocktail party. The good host will always be on the look-out for empty glasses and will always ask the guest, "May I?" before refilling a drink.

A host who values his furnishings would be wise to leave a tray or two positioned to receive used dishes. In order to prevent this space from looking like the refuse area in a fast-food restau-rant, the alert host will empty these trays before they become overloaded. Likewise, the consider-ate guest will search for a suitable place to leave his dinnerware before automatically abandoning it on the stereo.

Should you bring your cocktail glass to the dinner table or do you leave it behind even if it holds a freshly poured drink? This is not an earthshaking dilemma, but in the course of social events, it is a recurring one. When all is consid-ered, I must say that at a formal dinner one should automatically leave an unfinished cocktail behind. At an informal dinner, a guest may bring his cocktail to the dining table. Bear in mind, however, that this does not mean that the hostess is then obligated to keep refreshing the cocktail glass during the rest of the meal.

At a dinner party one should eat wisely but not too well, and talk well but not too wisely.

W. SOMERSET MAUGHAM

THE FINE ART OF CONVERSATION

Faith! He must make his

stories shorter

Or change his comrades once

a quarter.

JONATHAN SWIFT

Good conversation is the essence of any enjoyable dinner party. A host or hostess can plan a party perfectly down to the last detail, spending much time and considerable money, but without the energy and sizzle of the guests' conversation, the whole evening can turn into a lead-footed disaster. I have known many mediocre cooks who were regarded as great hosts or hostesses simply because of their talent for creating an atmosphere in which exciting conversation flourished. Even more so than the evening's tangible ingredients ~ the food, the wine, the setting ~ good talk is what makes an occasion interesting and exciting.

Artful conversation invites response. It is never a monologue or lecture, but is designed to evoke the enthusiastic interest and response of others. Accomplished hosts know how to make their guests shine in conversation. While it was once thought of as being the host's sole responsibility to orchestrate dinner conversation, today we can accept the democratic reality that this is an obligation shared with guests. Neither a talk-show host nor a parliamentarian designating each guest's allotted time to speak, a deft host keeps the tempo nicely paced by introducing topics known to be of interest, or topics on which the guests are knowledgeable. He can change the tone of the conversation when lighthearted intervention is needed and direct questions to shy guests or those he feels may have been neglected.

The successful guest, on the other hand, makes it a point to study the interests of his fellow guests, and to gauge the range of topics that may be boring or too controversial ~ religion, abortion, the death penalty, for example ~ and to note those subjects that are the most pleasing. There are literally thousands of topics appropriate for the dinner table; perennially popular are travel, hobbies, what is current in the arts, music, theater, museums, books, and so on. Sometimes a dollop of good old-fashioned gossip ~ kept within the bounds of fairness and good grace, of course ~ can fuel the most entertaining conversations. But at a dinner party made up of relative strangers, it is always wisest to keep to subjects of more general interest.

The tenor of conversation often changes as the evening progresses. The social dynamic begun over cocktails with general chatting about universal matters such as the weather, transportation, the nature of the occasion itself, may deepen as the party moves to the dinner table, taking on more intimacy. It is still wise, however, to steer away from extensive discussion and extreme positions. Do not become so wrapped up in arguing a point that you neglect your meal and paralyze your fellow diners.

Blessed is the man who,

having nothing to say,

abstains from giving us wordy

evidence of that fact.

GEORGE ELIOT

35

Keep your own counsel

Sure to dull any dinner party is the conversation of the bore. Wholly convinced of the fascination his life holds for others, he can make an evening seem endless. In the throes of such conversational captivity, suffering guests are entitled to requisition from their social arsenal a blind eye and a deaf ear. When the first guest starts to slide under the table, a gentle chiding may alert the bore to his trespass.

Be aware of the tastes of your audience. Do not use shockingly rude language if there is even the slightest chance it might offend. A nice bit of gossip, a "respectable" naughty joke, a slightly ribald story or experience ~ if told with delicacy and wit ~ are far more entertaining, and often can awaken an otherwise indifferent evening.

The same warning pertains to the use of slang. Believe it or not, some people still have respect for the English language and for other people. Please refrain from using slang, humorous or otherwise, unless you are certain it will amuse and not offend others at your gathering. Teenagers in particular need to be taught about not using their slang or "street talk" in company.

Couples who quarrel openly at parties or dinners are complete bores. Nobody wants to see an amateur production of *Who's Afraid of Virginia Woolf?* when they are supposed to be having fun.

Good breeding consists in concealing how much we think of ourselves and how little we think of the other person.

MARK TWAIN

Airing one's problems in public is for those who enjoy being exhibitionistic rather than civilized. A hostess has every right to draw the warring couple aside and firmly request a cease-fire.

COMPLIMENTS AND CRITICISMS

There is an art to giving compliments and to receiving them. The guest who expresses his admiration for the host's efforts with a light touch is the most believable, whereas the guest who gushes becomes tedious. Restrain yourself from overblown comments such as "This is the best London broil I've ever had" to more relevant compliments like "The meat in these crab cakes is so fantastic. Is it the first of the season?"

A host must not look for compliments. Never ask a guest, "Did you enjoy the food?" If he did, he should tell you so without being asked; if not, politeness would forbid him to say so anyway.

A word of warning: Take care not to carry discussions of the meal itself to extremes. Though few would deny the importance of fine ingredients and skillful preparation, even I shrink from such overblown praise of what, after all, is just one element of a pleasant evening.

On the other side of the ledger, one should never criticize, draw attention to, or make fun of

[Sociability is] the art of unlearning to be preoccupied with yourself.

OSKAR BLUMENTHAL

the eating habits of others in public. If you feel it is absolutely necessary to criticize family or friends, do so in private. In particular, I think it is tiresome to hear spouses and friends chiding one another at table. Admonitions such as "You're going to gain ten pounds if you have even one more bite" or "Remember your cholesterol" certainly do not endear anyone to the hard-working host, whose fondest hope is to see his food appreciated.

Also, think twice before saying anything about the food habits of those from other countries. What is considered civilized in one culture may be barbaric in another. To the Chinese it is proper to suck on the bones of chicken and other poultry. Americans have a different approach, but we cannot say that ours is any more "correct" than others.

A gentleman is one who never

hurts anyone's feelings

unintentionally.

OSCAR WILDE

THROWING DOWN THE GAUNTLET

What should a guest do if placed in the extreme position of being pointedly insulted by another guest? Is an offended guest ever in the right to walk out of a dinner or party?

The premise of socializing is that everyone is a friend of the host and that the peace of his home will not be violated. If the insult is so great that it is truly unbearable, and in the absence of a duel at dawn, the only action a guest may take is to remove himself from the proceedings with apologies to his host and the other guests.

Can a host ever properly ask a guest to leave? Yes. The highest duty of a host is to protect his guests. A guest who has revealed himself to be aggressive has revealed himself to be uncivilized. The host may be witty and adept and save the day, but in the last analysis he must bear the responsibility of asking an offensive guest to leave.

TABLE TALK

The ordinary ebb and flow of conversation at an informal gathering is such that guests may usually address the gathering as a whole and not feel as though they were orating. One should not monopolize the conversation, however, or throw one's body across a table or sofa to converse with someone who is at a distance.

When seated at table, the only people a guest is actually required to speak to are his immediate neighbors to the left and right. At a relaxed family-style dinner, either side may be spoken to first, by either a female or male guest. If you have forgotten your neighbor's name, please do not hesitate to say, "I was a little overwhelmed when we were introduced. Would you tell me your

A civil guest

Will no more talk all, than

eat all, the feast.

GEORGE HERBERT

Courtesy on one side only

lasts not long.

GEORGE HERBERT

name again?" If you are a reserved person, and do not feel comfortable speaking to groups in general, there is no requirement that you do so.

Rules are not as rigid as they once were for formal dinners. In the past a gentleman always started conversing with his companion to the right. Today one may address the person on one's right or left first without committing a faux pas.

CHIVALRY IS NOT DEAD

We all know that there have been tremendous strides made in the area of equality of the sexes. However, let it be said that gentlemen may still assist ladies to be seated comfortably at table: If you are a man to be seated next to a woman, you should withdraw her chair toward you to permit her to walk in front of it. As she starts to sit, gently slide the chair forward so that her bent legs will slip comfortably under the table.

VULGAR VICES

OVERDRINKING

The guest who is "overserved" is not only a social liability; he can be a legal one, too. When it begins to appear that a guest cannot hold his liquor and starts to make a fool of himself in front of others, a host should exercise as much

caution and authority as possible. He may summon and pay for a taxi to ensure a safe trip. Or
the offending drinker may be invited into another room and quietly asked to make it an early
night. In any event, the host should be firm. He
will have the overdrinker's thanks in the morning. But he should never discuss the incident
openly with other guests. They will only wonder
what will be said about them after *they* leave.

SMOKING

While many hosts would prefer to have no
smoking in their homes, I believe that traditional
rules of hospitality should be adhered to: If a
guest withdraws a cigarette, he should immediately be provided with an ashtray. One can always hope that a guest would not impose this
increasingly unpopular habit upon others, and
would at the very least solicit the permission and
indulgence of other guests. But unless someone
whose health would be seriously compromised is
present, I am afraid the polite host will just have
to tolerate it. I am personally not a defender of
cigarette smoking in public, but I think it is important that we bear in mind that smoking
started as a social activity. Cigarette smoking is
notoriously difficult to stop, and you should not
make your guests feel like walking health hazards
because of their addiction.

If you absolutely forbid smoking of any sort

O God, that men should put

an enemy in their mouths to

steal away their brains.

WILLIAM SHAKESPEARE

in your home, you may want to put out social fires before they start: Give your guests fair warning by mentioning this hard-and-fast rule when you issue your invitation. If they cannot refrain for long without smoking, it is considerate to provide an outdoor seating area for this purpose. Some etiquette guides go so far as to advise readers to place "No Smoking" signs in their homes. I think this is needlessly harsh and looks institutional, but the host does have the right to insist on his principles.

One other note of caution: Children often have strong antismoking views, so parents should be well advised to review the rules of hospitality with them before they are placed in a social situation with smokers.

Gone the way of the calling card is another old custom ~ the traditional brandy and cigars interlude after dinner when men and women separated for a period of time. This was an opportunity for male smokers to indulge in their habit without offending anyone else's sensibilities, the assumption of course being that men could tolerate these hearty odors. I don't see how this is a gender-related issue: Unpleasant smells are unpleasant smells. Perhaps it is better to save those odorous cigars for a moment of solitary contemplation ~ while writing your hostess a lovely thank-you note, for instance.

OVEREATING

One of the most basic rules of good table manners is to avoid piling an excess of food on your plate. I have an indelible memory of my training as a waiter at the Ecole Hôtelière, the professional school of the Swiss Hotel Keepers Association in Lausanne. I had an outstanding instructor, a proud and kind man of reasoned discipline named Conrad Tuor. I was enrolled in the service course, and one day, under his watchful eye, we started the midday table service. I was stationed behind a platter of mashed potatoes, and when I filled the plate of a second student with an overflowing spoon of mashed potatoes, M. Tuor frowned and turned to me. *"Monsieur Claiborne,"* he said, *"rien n'est plus vulgaire"* ("nothing is more vulgar"). Inside myself I cringed, and since that day when serving guests (or myself) with food I have always doled out relatively small portions. A good host or hostess will have enough food on hand so that a plate can be refilled a second time, according to the guest's own needs.

Should a guest be faced with an unfamiliar food that is not appealing, or one high on his list of dietary taboos, he can maintain his poise by taking a very small portion, or by declining without a long-winded explanation or a descent into coyness.

It also follows that one of the greatest social

A full belly doth not engender a subtle wit.

GEORGE PETTIE

43

gaffes is crowding food into the mouth, followed only by the transgression of speaking with a mouthful of food. Always chew with the mouth closed, and eat only small portions at a time. This is not being too fastidious. The game of "Show" has limited humorous appeal for most adults. Also, taking small bites reduces the risks of choking, which is truly a terrifying experience.

PUBLIC GROOMING

For anyone who needs to be told, applying makeup at table is in the worst possible taste. The dining table is not a vanity, nor is it a hair salon or massage parlor. Guests who need to "fix" their hair or makeup or take a seventh-inning stretch are advised to retire to the nearest bathroom for such personal attention. There they may run hands through their hair, crack knuckles, and brush their jackets before returning to the table. Ladies in particular may wish to remember that the all-male after-dinner ritual of brandy and cigars does not leave a vacuum to be filled with a carillon of compacts and lipstick cases opening and closing.

Everyone thinks himself

well-bred.

LORD SHAFTESBURY

BODY LANGUAGE

Body language speaks volumes about us, perhaps no more eloquently so than in social situations. While to some people dissecting these nuances of behavior may seem a petty waste of time, let me assure you that we are all on view, and that our comportment and personal habits are key indicators of how others will think of us. I am not suggesting that we take refinement to absurd heights; I am suggesting that some common practices ~ some rather gross ones, I am afraid ~ must be eliminated in a mannerly society. If what follows seem like points of basic, decent behavior that are already incorporated into your life, then you have my admiration. If not, I hope this will help you avoid any awkward moments.

[Charm is] smiles and soap.

LEWIS CARROLL

Just as there are fundamental niceties that one automatically observes in public, there are fundamental prohibitions of behavior that one would not wish to witness even from one's worst enemy. Some of these I hesitate even to name; some I list below as quietly and discreetly as possible.

A FORK IS JUST A FORK

The awful habit of playing with one's silverware is obtrusive and distracting ~ and it may also speak of a nervous and inattentive personality. It can leave unattractive marks on the silverware, the sight of which would be an additional burden for other guests to bear.

While we are on the subject of silverware, it is hard to imagine anyone doing the following because it is so tasteless, but unfortunately be-

cause I have seen it done, I mention it here ~
turning one's knife or fork into a nail file and
cleaning one's nails with it. It is such an enormous violation of good manners that it would
leave a hard-to-overcome stain on one's social
reputation. The place for a manicure is at home,
where the offensive guest will find himself night
after night would he do such a thing in the pres-
ence of others.

TOOTH ACHES

Is it obvious that it is in the poorest taste to
clean one's teeth in public? In this country it is.
While in some Asian and European cultures it
may be considered proper to pick away at the
teeth behind a hand covering the mouth, it is
never so here.

In company, it is never acceptable to use any
object ~ toothpicks, the tines of a fork, match-
book covers, dental floss, a piece of jewelry ~ to
remove something irksome from your teeth. The
proper place to do this is in the bathroom. I am
certain your host will have one.

BABY TALK

What is the polite term for a guest to use
when asking directions to the toilet? In a private
home, the safe choices would include bathroom,
powder room, possibly washroom. Please do not

More tears have been shed

over men's lack of manners

than their lack of morals.

HELEN HATHAWAY

ever embarrass yourself by asking for the little girls' or little boys' room.

OUT ON A LIMB

Speaking of childlike . . . it is a small point, but I find it too casual when a guest sits with legs crossed under the table. It is a much more adult statement to keep the soles of both feet on the floor in a relaxed manner. This posture, in contrast to the more *boulevardier* habit of crossing one's legs, conveys the message that you are in control of yourself and in harmony with others at the table.

A man's own good-breeding

is his best security against

other people's ill manners.

LORD CHESTERFIELD

In general, it is best to keep one's elbows and arms off the table. There are times when elbow-resting is permissible ~ if, for instance, the meal is very casual and you are in the company of close friends, you may properly rest your arms and elbows on the edge of the table. Be careful, however, that this position does not lead to your intruding on another's space or knocking something over. If the meal is absolutely formal, keep your hands resting in your lap when you are not engaged in eating.

A DAB WILL DO

There is another small matter that amazingly enough some people still haven't realized is socially important, and that is the correct way to wipe food and liquid from the mouth. The refined person trains himself to always wipe his mouth before drinking a beverage, before speaking, and certainly if he feels food on his face. The proper way is to dab a napkin or tissue to your lips and the corners of your mouth. Do not wipe or scrub with unseemly vigor.

If you notice that the rim of your glass is conspicuously stained with food or wine, wipe away the offending marks with your napkin as casually as possible.

Even in the case of an unexpected dribble, never wipe your face with the back or front of your hand. It is a rare host or hostess who does not provide a guest with a napkin, so there is never an excuse for not using one.

ACCIDENTS WILL HAPPEN

A host is like a general:

it takes a mishap to reveal

his genius.

HORACE

What if a guest drops a glass or accidentally shatters a treasured vase? The valiant host remains calm. He will sweep up the shards as if nothing happened and continue the conversation, showing no hint of anger or resentment. Expressing negative emotions would reveal him to be insensitive to his guest's feelings. And we all know that accidents do happen to everyone. The guest is not under an obligation to replace the broken object, nor to make an endless fuss over offering to do so. She should simply express her apologies, and perhaps do so again in her thank-you note or phone call.

What if a guest spills wine or other liquid at the table? If it is a small spill the guest may quickly dab it away with his napkin. If the spill is large and conspicuous, the hostess may wish to cover it with another napkin.

GUEST OR EMPLOYEE?

For a guest to offer to help a host or hostess is one of those great no-win situations. Should the host decline, the guest can wonder if she has been offensive, implying that the host could not handle everything. And if the host should accept, then the poor guest is put to work.

The gesture has become so trite that it is like saying, "Have a nice day." If a guest really comes to a dinner party eager to help the host or hostess, she will arrive in a good mood, prepared to enjoy herself. That is the biggest help she can offer her host.

Sweet courtesy has done

it most

If you have made

each guest forget

That he himself is not

the host.

THOMAS BAILEY ALDRICH

CHAPTER THREE

Table settings
and unsettings

The pleasure in eating is

not in the costly flavor,

but in yourself.

HORACE

The sensory pleasure of dining is hardly limited to the taste of the food; imagine, if you can, the diminished enjoyment of a superbly seasoned, delicately poached salmon served in the plastic environment of a fast-food establishment. A fine table, with its spotless crystal, softly polished silverware, and sparkling plates poised upon an impeccable damask cloth, demonstrates an accomplished host's pride of place and promises his guests a superior evening. Whenever I see such a table, I completely give myself over to the spirit of the evening ahead. Elegance and graciousness do indeed still have a place in the dining room.

DECORATING STYLE

The successful host employs an artist's eye when dressing his table, whether his style is opulent, creative, or very down-to-earth. Urns of extravagant flowers or elaborate candelabra are, by polite standards, overdoing it. A great bowl filled to the brim with sunny lemons or baby artichokes would be far more captivating. I always look forward to sitting at the table that belongs to a friend who loves to scour flea markets and roadside antique stores for quirky, interesting objects for her table settings. Beyond the meal itself, she treats her guests to a visual and tactile feast; her whimsical creations never fail to spark humorous exchanges and greater intimacy. And they are always far more eloquent than overwrought four-hundred-dollar flower arrangements.

Resist the temptation to make your table setting the living embodiment of your ego, or a statement about your income. Your first consideration should be the comfort of your guests. Look carefully ~ is there anything on the table that could hamper the easy flow of conversation? If the answer is yes, it should be removed immediately; this will also prevent a situation in which a guest requests that you do so, which is entirely within his rights.

BURNING YOUR CANDLES

Candles and centerpieces should be about two inches below the eye level of your guests. A candle flame flickering between your gaze and the person across the table is annoying, not romantic. I like to light the candles just before my guests are seated, and allow them to burn until everyone stands. White or ivory tapers are appropriate for any table, and of course they should be free of any fragrance. Incidentally, it is excessive to burn candles during sunny, daylight hours; they should be lit only at dusk, or later, or on overcast days when the table might otherwise be

Manners must adorn knowledge, and smooth its way through the world. Like a great rough diamond, it may do very well in a closet by way of curiosity, and also for its intrinsic value; but it will never be worn, nor shine, if it is not polished.

LORD CHESTERFIELD

gloomy. To extinguish a candle flame, use a long-handled candle snuffer. If you are obliged to blow out a candle, hold your cupped hand behind the flame so as to prevent spraying hot wax on your linens.

Some manuals on etiquette recommend that the tips of new candles be burned an inch or so to remove the "newness" from them before being placed on the table. Personally, I find clean, unburned pristine wicks more appealing.

PLACE SETTINGS

Although a great many people boast of their sophisticated palates, an equally great number of individuals are, in fact, uninformed about the correct use of silverware, dinnerware, and glasses. I concede that this subject may be less "creative" than the art of cooking itself, but the proper place setting not only makes a dinner look more attractive, it can actually make dining easier. As a part of the social language you share with your guests, it is incumbent upon you to learn the basics so you can demonstrate your skill with fluency.

In the most formal dining circumstances, a table setting would begin with a service plate of fine china. These large plates, usually twelve inches in diameter, act as a base for all courses served during the meal, and as such they remain on the table until the last of the meal, including the coffee service, has been finished.

Service plates can of course be used for less than formal dinners as well. If they are not in your china repertoire, you should be certain that the space on the table in front of each guest is not left endlessly empty between courses. Remember, your first goal as a host is to keep guests stimulated during the meal.

Place every plate with care so that any motifs or monograms are in the same position and are easy to discern. Plates for each course should be situated on the service plate as neatly and uniformly as possible so that the food "faces" each diner in the same way. At dessert, for example, wedges of pie and cake should point toward the diner. With all the dishes you will use at table, mixed patterns are infinitely preferable to matched plates that are scarred with chips or cracks. There are few sights more depressing than a teacup with a crudely mended handle or a stack of chipped saucers: Throw them away.

SIDE DISHES

Even at a casual meal, a good host will spare guests the discomfort of having several courses heaped on a single plate. Each place setting should include a smaller plate for bread and one for salad. Place the bread plate to the left of the

Manners are more important

than laws. Upon them,

in a great measure, the

laws depend.

EDMUND BURKE

dinner plate so that it is close to the tines of the fork that is farthest to the left. Place the salad plate diagonally to the upper left of the dinner plate. These two smaller plates should almost touch. If salad or an appetizer is to be served as a separate course, that plate should be placed directly on the service plate.

Place cut-up sections of butter in a small dish, then place this dish on top of a slightly larger flat underdish. Serve the butter with a fork ~ a cocktail fork is ideal for spearing the pats. Butter knives are unnecessary; they are unwieldy, and often the butter pats roll off the knife blade, causing needless embarrassment. Guests serve themselves, then return the fork to the underdish before passing the dish on.

Butter served at the table may be molded or curled into fancy shapes, or sliced into pats. If you refrigerate the pats until mealtime, they will remain firm and separate and will be easier to serve. Please do not place butter on a bowl of crushed ice; it is really a silly affectation that does not belong in the home.

[Eating is that which explains] half the emotion of life.

SYDNEY SMITH

WASTE DISHES

Many foods generate an extraordinary amount of debris in the process of being eating ~ lobster, clams, crab in the shell, artichokes, corn on the cob, poultry, just to name a few. Unless you want your guests to feel as though their plates were laden with landfill, it is best to furnish them with small side dishes to the left of the dinner plate, above the bread plate.

THE SILVER STANDARD

Employing inappropriate silverware for a dinner party is tantamount to dressing tastelessly for the occasion. Formal silver at a casual dinner is vulgar, rather like showing off one's jewelry, while everyday silver at a formal party is like the cliché gesture of mixing black tie and sneakers. I probably set out my best silver only three or four times a year; my everyday pattern is elegant and versatile enough for most meals I host. There is no need to overwhelm guests with a militant parade of cutlery. The number of utensils for each diner, and their placement, are based on simple logic dictated by the courses to be served and the order in which they will appear.

Place forks on the left of the plate in order of usage: The first one farthest from the plate is the one to be used first. The same principle applies to knives: Place one for each course on the right of the service or dinner plate. The one to be used first is farthest from the plate. When soup is served as a first course, place the soup spoon to

They dined on mince, with

slices of quince

which they ate with a

runcible spoon.

And hand in hand on the

edge of the sand

They danced by the light of

the moon.

EDWARD LEAR

the right of the knife that is at the extreme right. A small butter knife should rest on the bread dish's upper left rim, with the blade facing the diner. Coffee spoons are not placed on the table at the beginning of the meal; they are served on the coffee cup saucers when coffee is poured at the end of the meal.

DESSERT CUTLERY

If your meal has more than three courses, a dessert fork and spoon ~ and more delicate than the regular silverware ~ can be placed directly above the dinner plate, arranged horizontally: fork facing right, spoon above the fork, facing left. You can also put dessert silver and plates on the table after dinner, just before dessert is served, with the fork to the left and the spoon to the right. With some desserts, a fork may suffice; in such a case it should be placed to the right of the plate ~ simple logic again, since it is the same utensil and will be picked up in the right hand in the majority of cases. A dessert knife, which would be used to peel fresh fruit, would also be placed to the right of the plate.

CHOPSTICKS

When serving an Oriental meal, do give your guests the choice of silverware or chopsticks. Chopstick rests should also be provided. In Chinese tradition they are placed to the right of

He who endeavors to please

must appear pleased.

SAMUEL JOHNSON

the dinner plate and level with the upper rim, chopsticks vertical. Japanese custom situates the rests in front and to the left of the dinner plate, chopsticks horizontal.

SERVING DISHES

As courses are served, sauces, gravies, and vinaigrettes prepared especially for particular dishes are placed on the table in bowls. For me, nothing makes a table look more like a delicatessen than condiments served in their jars and bottles; they should be decanted into attractive containers. In many instances it may seem as though their packaging has become part of their identity ~ ketchup and salad dressing are two examples ~ but only under very informal circumstances should these be served in their original bottles or jars. Picnics and informal family meals are two exceptions; indeed, for many breakfasts the battery of pitchers for juices, milk, and cream; bowls for cereals, jams and jellies, sugar and its substitutes; and spoons and underdishes required would result in breakfast served quite late in the morning.

Glass pitchers are perfect for cream and syrups. Preserves, chutney, relishes, mustards, and seasoning sauces such as ketchup, Tabasco, and Worcestershire should be presented in indi-

Behavior is a mirror in which

everyone shows his image.

JOHANN WOLFGANG

VON GOETHE

vidual decorative dishes, preferably small shallow bowls, with underdishes large enough to hold small serving spoons, which are placed to the right of the bowl. If you are hosting a large group, you may wish to put out two or more sets of condiments to reduce the traffic and allow your guests to dine in peace. Remove with all other extraneous dishes before dessert.

Forms keep fools at a

distance.

SAMUEL FOOTE

At very informal meals only, where the host loves to share the experience of cooking, fresh cheese may be grated at the table, with the aid of an immaculate cheese mill, or simply a metal grater resting on a plate. At other gatherings, already grated cheese should be served in a small bowl, complete with an underdish and a small serving spoon.

SALT AND PEPPER

The service of salt and pepper is up to the discretion of the host. If you do not wish to place salt and pepper on the table, plan to have them nearby in case of request.

You may pour salt and pepper into small bowls, or use matching salt and pepper mills. Make sure to provide at least one salt and one pepper container for every two guests. Nothing is more maddening than a constant roundelay of requests for these seasonings. If you are using the type of mills that are likely to leave grains on your tablecloth, put them on an underdish.

If as a guest you find a small individual salt dish in front of your plate, with no accompanying salt spoon, this is an indication that your host expects you to serve yourself a small amount with a pinch of your fingers.

CRYSTAL

At a minimum, crystal at an elegant dinner should include stemmed glasses for wine and water. Wineglasses have a tapered bowl, while water goblets are rounder and flatter where the bowl meets the stem. No order-of-usage maxims prevail with stemware: Set the taller glasses toward the center of the table, and the water goblets just above the knife at the right. If each place setting is to have more than these two kinds of glasses ~ say a short fluted glass for sherry ~ others should be set to the right of the water goblet. The main idea is not to obscure smaller glasses with larger ones.

Put out separate wineglasses for each different wine you plan to serve during the entire meal except for dessert wine; these make an appearance with the dessert service. If you plan to serve champagne as your dessert wine, place champagne glasses on the table from the beginning.

Too great refinement is false delicacy, and true delicacy is solid refinement.

LA ROCHEFOUCAULD

I wish it were unnecessary to state that glassware should be impeccably spotless; many hosts thoughtlessly overlook this aesthetic and hygienic point. Even heavy-duty commercial dishwashers may fail to remove spots, so each glass should be wiped with a lint-free cotton or linen cloth, then set by its stem upon the table.

NAPKINS

A diplomat is a person who can tell you to go to hell in such a way that you actually look forward to the trip.

CASKIE STINNETT

If a single element could be said to elevate the ambience of a given meal, it may very well be the cloth or linen napkin. Or perhaps it is the opposite that is truer ~ the most exquisitely orchestrated dinner will stagger with the appearance of paper napkins. There are two sizes of the cloth/linen version ~ the American napkin is the size of a lap; the European one is about the size of a good bed pillow. Both are adequate and proper (the European perhaps more than adequate) provided they are all-cotton or linen, snowy white and spotless, and pressed smooth.

Set the napkin either to the left of the fork or directly on the service plate. How it is folded is basically unimportant, provided all the napkins are folded in a uniform manner. This should be simple, neat, appealing to the eye, easily accessible, and easy to unfold. Stuffing the napkin into a water glass so that it fans out in a pattern of exploding pleats borders on the pompous and increases the chances of toppling the glass when it is removed.

Napkin rings have long been an accepted part of all but the most formal table settings. I associate them mainly with dining *en famille*, where, for reasons of practicality, family members use one cloth napkin for a period of time, refolding it after each meal and putting it back in its ring. If you choose to use napkin rings, simple is always best ~ smooth wood or silver, for example. Neatly folded napkins in their rings go to the left of the service plate.

A CLEAR COURSE

Before dessert is served, the table should be cleared completely of dishes used for previous courses; this includes salt and pepper mills, wineglasses (unless champagne is the dessert wine, in which case the champagne glasses remain in place), and condiment dishes.

CHAPTER FOUR

LET THE MEAL BEGIN

While announcing that "Dinner is served" may be a reminder of a more opulent era when butlers and vast wealth seemed to be in great supply, it sounds a bit strained, and certainly anachronistic, in these days of comparative informality. A simple "Shall we eat?" or "Let's go into dinner" is more than adequate for any modern-day host. Please forget any thoughts of dinner gongs, triumphal music, or four-year-olds screaming "Soup's on!"

HONOR THY GUESTS

The great secret is not having good manners or bad manners or any particular sort of manners, but having the same manners for all human souls.

GEORGE BERNARD SHAW

If a couple is hosting a dinner party, the host should be the first to move toward the dining table with a female guest ~ the guest of honor if there is one. The hostess is usually the last to go in, after making sure everyone else is informed of dinner. Her proper place is at the opposite end of the table from the host. The single host or hostess should take the place at the head of the table, to be in a position to observe the needs of all of his or her guests.

Many etiquette books state that the guest of honor should be seated either to the right of the host or opposite him at the foot of the table. As I stated earlier, I personally prefer to give an honored guest the place that commands the best view of the room.

66

NAPKINS REVISITED

The right moment to place a napkin on the lap is immediately after sitting down at the table, not when food arrives. The only exception would be at a very formal dinner, when guests usually wait for the hostess to position hers before unfolding theirs. To place a napkin on your lap, simply unfold it. Do not whip it around like a flag at a racetrack. If it is too generously sized for your comfort, leave it folded in half.

If during dinner you need to excuse yourself from the table for any reason, place the napkin gently to the left of your dinner plate. Do not refold it or throw it in a heap on a chair like dirty laundry. If your plate has been cleared, leave the napkin on the table in front of you. Please note that when laying aside a napkin, the knowledgeable person makes certain that all visible parts are clean in appearance ~ that is to say, not soiled with food or stained with lipstick.

At a very formal gathering where there may be professional service, an observant waiter or waitress will pick up a fallen napkin for a guest and replace it, just as he or she would do in a fine restaurant. If this is not the case, however, it is perfectly acceptable for the guest to lean over unobtrusively and retrieve it himself.

At the end of a meal, if all the dishes from your place setting have been removed, casually put your napkin ~unfolded ~ on the table directly in front of you. If a dessert plate remains in front of you, place your unfolded napkin to the right of it.

Only in very specific circumstances should guests ~ male or female ~ entertain the notion of tucking a napkin into a shirt front. If you are a guest at a crab feast or picnic, for instance, it makes perfect sense to protect yourself this way. It is never proper at more formal gatherings.

If you are dining *en famille*, complete with napkin rings, there is no need to roll the napkin and place it back in the ring unless you anticipate being present at the next meal. Empty napkin rings are placed above and to the left of the dinner plate during the meal.

[Charm is] the ability to make someone else think that both of you are wonderful.

EDGAR MAGNIN

TO YOUR HEALTH

A toast may be offered during any course of the meal, but since it is best to wait until all your guests have laid down their forks and knives, this may be a challenge to coordinate. The most propitious times for making toasts are just before the meal begins or after the dessert course. It is perfectly proper to tap on a wineglass to get everyone's attention. Serving should be suspended while a toast is being spoken. The person offering the toast should rise; he does not have to be holding his wineglass. At a formal gathering everyone but the person being toasted should rise. At the end of the toast maker's words, guests raise their glasses, then take a small sip of wine. The person being honored does not join in that first sip of wine, but waits until others are finished with the toast. Then he may stand if he wishes and make a brief reply. In days gone by, men being so honored traditionally offered back a toast. Today it is acceptable for both male and female guests to do so, or to remain seated and lift their glasses in acknowledgment of the tribute.

What does a person who does not drink alcoholic beverages do during a toast? She may raise an empty glass, or in anticipation of the toast request a soft drink or water to be poured into her glass instead. The farsighted host will have considered this possibility beforehand if he knows the drinking preferences of his guests.

Incidentally, more than one toast may be made during a meal. Often this can lead to much hilarity, although as subsequent toasts ensue, it is less necessary ~ and considerably more challenging ~ to rise to one's feet with each one.

Friendship cannot live without ceremony, nor without civility.
LORD HALIFAX

SERVING DIRECTIONS

Without exception, dishes are served from the left and cleared from the right. All serving

A life of pleasure requires an

aristocratic setting to make it

interesting.

GEORGE SANTAYANA

platters are presented from the left as well, accompanied by serving silver. Glasses, however, are always presented from the right.

At a family-style meal, where serving dishes are brought to the table by the host, guests should pass these dishes among themselves, starting with the guest on the host's right. If a dish or platter is especially heavy, the guest passing should hold the platter as the guest on his right serves himself. Then this guest would do the same for the person next to him.

At a larger meal ~ say, for ten ~ it would be considerate for a host to provide two platters of the main entrée. This would ensure that those on the end of the serving route receive hot food. The host may start one platter to his right, the other to his left.

Once the food has been passed, guests should feel free to begin eating, although most people prefer to wait until the host signals them to do so. At a large gathering, the perceptive host will encourage guests to begin eating after he notices that three or four people have already been served. The skillful host keeps a watch on the activities at the table and attempts to time the courses accordingly.

When all the guests are finished with each course ~ and only then ~ the host may clear the dishes. The civilized way to do this is by removing one dish at a time in each hand and carrying them off to the kitchen. This process may be time-consuming, but scraping dishes at the table and lugging them away in wobbly stacks is a sight that can spoil the mood of the evening, and is to my mind much too "shirtsleeves" for any dining occasion.

At the very end of the meal, after coffee has been served at the table, the host may remove the coffee cups, saucers, and spoons and leave the liqueur glasses on the table until after his guests have left.

TEMPERATE ACTS

Among the most common kitchen-to-table errors committed by hosts is improperly serving hot and cold foods. There is no mystery in doing it properly. Hot foods, especially hot soups, should always be served on hot plates; cold foods belong on cold ones. By cold I mean less than room temperature but not freezing. Certain foods belong on well-chilled plates. Caviar, for example, is much better when spooned onto a chilled plate. So are gelatin desserts such as charlottes and mousselike mixtures. Sometimes it is preferable to chill dishes for ice cream and sherbet in the freezer before serving.

On the other hand, take care to see that plates are not overheated: They might crack. An

I am very grateful to old age because it has increased my desire for conversation and lessened my desire for food and drink.

CICERO

electric warming oven specially designed for warming plates may be a bit costly for most kitchens, but they do heat several dozen plates of various sizes in compact space. The "dry" setting on a dishwasher accomplishes the same effect.

When taking in an extremely hot plate or bowl from kitchen to table, use a clean napkin or cloth to protect your fingers. Never use a shredded kitchen towel or burned mitten. (Mittens, by the way, are rarely if ever used by professional chefs; they tend to prefer heavy kitchen towels, usually folded, to prevent burns.)

Certain dishes served at a buffet require special attention: If a hot soup is the first or second course, pour it into the tureen or bowl at the last moment before guests are called. Again, make sure the soup bowls are hot.

While not essential, it is a thoughtful gesture on the part of hosts to warm coffee cups before serving. A common method is to run the cups under the hot water tap, draining and wiping them dry just before they are used.

Welcome in your eye, your

hand, your tongue.

WILLIAM SHAKESPEARE

FINGER BOWLS

It is true that in this day and age finger bowls may seem as obsolescent as corsets or opera glasses, but they are, nonetheless, one of the most refined accessories on anyone's dining table.

They are a logical and elegant device for allowing diners to clean up at table and comfortably continue with their meal.

To prepare one, partially fill a small bowl with lukewarm water and, if you wish, float a leaf, such as a rose or geranium leaf, or very thin lemon slice in the water. Place a doily, preferably cloth, on a medium-size plate and top that with another saucer designed to hold the finger bowl. Then place the finger bowl in the center of this saucer, and place a napkin, neatly folded, on the rim of the bowl. (If you have never carried one into the dining room, you might want to practice before your meal.)

To use a finger bowl, take the napkin off the bowl and place it to the left of the saucer. Dip your fingers in the water gently and swish them around; wipe with the napkin, casually fold it, and replace it on the rim of the bowl.

If you do not wish to use finger bowls, you might offer hand towels instead. Present a tray or basket with neatly rolled hand towels that have been dampened slightly with warm water. Once used, they should be returned to the basket or tray for removal.

In either event, please do not encumber your guests with perfumed napkins or water. Perfumes violate the senses at a meal, are in terrible taste, and smack of the so-called VIP treatment on commercial airlines.

At table, I prefer the witty

before the grave…in bed,

beauty before goodness; and

in common discourse,

eloquence, whether or not

there be sincerity.

MONTAIGNE

NEATNESS COUNTS

It is an inescapable fact of dining that foods sometimes wind up on a tablecloth. When you wish to spoon a sauce onto your dinner plate, move the sauce container close to the plate before lifting the spoon. If this is unfeasible, lift your plate close to the sauce. If you are serving a table companion, hold a small plate under your spoon as you serve.

Coffee cups and teacups are notorious for spilling. Like ships in a storm, they toss their contents with abandon, leaving guests to wonder what to do with the puddle in their saucer. Of course, you may request a clean saucer, but failing that, the only thing to do is quietly pour the spilled coffee back into your cup. If there is a napkin nearby, you may dry the saucer with it.

The more the merrier ~ the

fewer the better fare.

JOHN HAYWOOD

A QUESTION OF APPETITE

If a guest at your table asks to be served small portions of food throughout the meal, accede to his wishes rather than trying to prove there is more than enough food. Of course, the concept of what a small portion is varies from person to person; what may be minuscule to one can be excessive to another. Ideally, if a serving platter is not passed from guest to guest, you should serve each portion and ask each guest if the offered amount is sufficient. It is far more gracious to add than to take away.

On the opposite hand, there are those guests who cannot seem to get enough. I have to admit that I am always charmed by their type of enthusiasm. I anticipate requests for second and even third helpings and have extra servings available. A host should simply inquire if anyone would care for more. A guest who takes him up on his offer then passes his plate, placing his silverware securely on top if it. If the dish he desires is already on the table near him, he may serve himself.

HOLDING FORK

It is absolutely astonishing how many people do not know the most elementary techniques for holding silverware. Fortunately, it is not at all difficult to handle cutlery correctly. There are two basic techniques: One is American, the other European. Although both are perfectly acceptable, to my mind the American style is less efficient, and can appear clumsy.

In the American method, hold the fork in your left hand and point the tines downward with your index finger, pressing lightly as your other fingers wrap around the base. Spear the food in the center with the fork tines using just

Manners make the man.

DANIEL DEFOE

enough pressure to keep it in place, then slice down with a cutting motion with the knife you are holding neatly enclosed in the palm of your right hand. After cutting off a bite-size portion, rest the knife on the rim of your plate (with the blade pointing inward toward the center); transfer the fork, tine upward, with the speared food, to the right hand; and, finally, eat.

In the European style, the food is cut as in the American style, but the knife, blade pointing down, remains in the right hand, and the fork with the food remains in the left. While eating, you may rest the knife on the right rim of your plate, or you may hold it; the fork may be placed tines down on the left side of the plate.

Whatever style you select, do not clench a utensil as if it were a dagger. And try to use your silverware as noiselessly as possible. The loud clatter of a knife tapping against a plate betrays a lack of finesse.

To rest your silverware on your plate before you have finished a course ~ to use a napkin or pick up a glass, for example ~ place the tips of the knife and fork near the top of the plate, the handles out to either side, forming an inverted V. The fork tines should be facing down. To indicate you have finished a course, place the knife and fork in the center of the plate, parallel and close together. Let the handles of the silverware rest on the plate rim at "twenty-minutes-past-

[Etiquette is] the art of

wearing appropriate masks.

MAX GRALNICK

76

the-hour" position, and the tips rest on the plate at "ten-minutes-before." Do not place silverware in a manner indicating you are finished with that particular course if you are not. Also, do not commit the unsightly error of resting your silverware on top of uneaten food. Discreetly push the food remnants to the side of the dish to make room for the knife and fork.

A spoon should rest on the underplate to the right of a bowl or cup when you are finished with the course as a signal that you are done. If there is no underplate, leave your spoon positioned in the center of the bowl. Under no circumstances should used silverware be placed on a service plate.

Should you be served a course that requires a fork, knife, and a spoon ~ a bouillabaisse, for example ~ after eating, arrange the silverware close to and parallel to each other on the underplate ~ fork on the left, knife and spoon to the right. Rest the handles on the plate rim, with the tines and tips slightly above the center of the plate.

Above all strive, within reason, to keep all silverware clean-looking as it is being used. For instance, if you are eating ice cream, be sure to consume the entire portion you have taken on your spoon in the trip to your mouth; sucking on the bowl over the course of several trips is extraordinarily unappetizing to witness.

Let us be very strange and very well-bred: Let us be as strange as if we had been married a good while, and as well-bred as if we were not married at all.

WILLIAM CONGREVE

POURING WINE

Wineglasses should be filled half to two thirds full. In my experience guests who drink wine at meals generally enjoy more than one glass, so it is the observant host who notices if his guests need a refill before they start to wonder "What do I have to do to get a drink around here?" The elegant approach is for the host to inquire, "May I?" while holding the wine bottle expectantly. This is far better than asking, "Would you like more wine?" If the guest accepts, the host pours the wine directly into the wineglass without lifting up the guest's glass or putting his hands on it, as fingerprints could soil the glass and lessen the guest's pleasure of a fine wine.

A simple "No, thank you" will suffice if one wishes to decline a refill. Under no circumstances should one cover the glass with the palm of the hand. This is an inappropriate gesture unworthy of a sophisticated individual.

Again, as stated earlier, wine is poured from a guest's right. Wineglasses should be removed from the right as well.

If you are serving a wine that you would like to showcase ~ a special vintage, or a wine chosen for a celebration such as a birthday, for example ~ it is considered in good taste to hold the bottle, label side up, to let your guests know what they are drinking.

A night of good drinking

Is worth a year's thinking.

CHARLES COTTON

Soup's on

Soups are served in either soup cups or shallow soup plates. The customary way to eat soup is to lift the rim of the soup plate nearest you at a slight angle; this causes the soup to recede to the opposite end of the bowl, where it can then be taken up with a spoon. I must point out that to my mind the technique of lifting up the rim of the bowl from the far end is equally proper. It is also a good idea to decorously lean forward ever so slightly to allow any misguided drops to fall back into the soup dish.

A soup spoon should be placed on the underplate if the rim is large enough to accommodate it. Otherwise, it belongs inside the bowl.

Breaking bread

I serve bread in simple bread baskets lined with immaculately clean white cloths. I like to offer guests long or medium-length loaves, sliced, or at least partly sliced, to facilitate handling. When you are offered bread, take only as much as you feel you will eat. It is never correct to take a large portion, break off a piece, and return the remainder to the basket. This would be handling someone else's food, which is unpleasant to say the least.

Politeness is the art of choosing among one's real thoughts.

ABEL STEVENS

In all likelihood the bread basket will be offered to you by someone on your right, and it is intended to be passed around clockwise. Take the basket in one hand while removing the bread with the other. Even if you do not want any, you should, as a matter of courtesy, take the basket and pass it to the person sitting to your left. After everyone has been served, the basket should be placed back on the table. If a waiter is serving, it is not necessary for you to touch the basket; just reach in and remove the piece you have chosen.

Once on your bread plate, break the bread into bite-size pieces, which are to be buttered individually. The exception may be hot breads, where it makes sense to butter the entire piece at once so the butter will melt.

COFFEE AND LIQUEURS

Coffee and after-dinner cordials, or liqueurs, are the traditional finish to a meal. It is a matter of personal taste, but I am of the opinion that the term "after-dinner" coffee means precisely that ~ coffee should not be served until after the dessert course. (Wines, sparkling and otherwise, should be served throughout dessert.) Shortly before you do serve coffee, place the sugar and creamer set on the table.

I believe you must always use freshly brewed

coffee, and I feel it is most elegantly served in demi-tasse cups. Make sure that the cup handle faces the right side, as most people are right-handed, or to the left if you remember that your guest is left-handed.

FINAL ACTS

It is perhaps a marginal note in the world of manners, but I feel it is worth considering the appearance of food on one's plate after a meal is finished. The components of a course ~ meat or fish, vegetable, and so on ~ should be neatly separated in piles. This is so easily done, and it does matter to the sensitive eye that food not be mashed about and look like rubbish. Where appearances are concerned, a guest does not want to risk hurting the host's feelings by leaving behind a mess that that might imply contempt for the food on which she has just dined.

It is also a worthwhile reminder that to push one's plate away after eating is a discourteous gesture. Other guests who know better will be kind enough to overlook this telling breach of etiquette, but my advice to anyone guilty of this bad habit has to break it immediately.

There is nothing better for a man; that he should eat and drink, and that he should make his soul enjoy good his labor.

ECCLESIASTES 11:24

CHAPTER FIVE

The restaurant
adventure

Outside the home, a good meal with friends in a restaurant may be our sole occasion of nourishing social relations in an age of lethal pressures, instant communications, and deadlines. As such, this respite from the slings and arrows of daily misfortune ought to be thoroughly enjoyable and relaxed, sparked by scintillating company and food. Incredibly, even in the finest restaurants, I have seen inexcusable manners sour a memorable repast, and have wondered at celebrated patrons draped in *haute couture* who perpetrate the basest incivility and thoughtlessness toward fellow diners. Unless you are sequestered in an establishment's private dining room, no restaurant is a fitting venue for exhibition of startling psychodramas or unresolved Oedipal complexes.

THE PLACE IS THE THING

It should be obvious that when planning a dinner party in a restaurant, the tastes and comfort of guests ~ as well as expense, particularly if more than one person is to contribute to the bill ~ are one's first imperative. Consider visiting an establishment in advance to examine its menu in order to determine if it is the best choice for your gathering. In fact it would be an exceptional stroke to present yourself in person to the maître d' when making that reservation for a special dinner. This will practically assure superior attention from the staff.

Certainly the diner has infinite choice today in gratifying the palate. In my salad days, when I first sampled lamb couscous in Casablanca and *cha gio* in Saigon, I hardly imagined such culinary treasure would become common fare in my neighborhood restaurants. Now that this globalism is a fact, it is both gracious and astute to take into consideration the extent of your guests' exotic tastes, and to solicit reaction to your choice before making a reservation.

Conduct is three-fourths of our life and its largest concern.

MATTHEW ARNOLD

A CLOTHES CALL

I recall the era when Henri Soulé was the country's premier restaurateur at Manhattan's Le Pavillon. If a gentleman appeared for dinner after six in the evening wearing any shoes other than black ones, he was banished to the bar for at least an hour before being seated.

While the days when dressing for dinner meant glamorous formal attire are long gone, it is still *de rigueur* for gentlemen to don dark suits and discreet ties in grander dining establishments. Similarly I find that the most elegant women rarely call attention to their flawless apparel. They choose understated clothing and jewelry ~ and perfume ~ suitable to the occasion where food and company, not egotism, reign. If you entertain any doubt as to a restaurant's dress code, phone in advance to determine its requirements.

SHADES OF PRETENTIOUSNESS

Do we have Hollywood or New York City to thank for the affectation of wearing sunglasses indoors? And after the sun has set as well! Unless it is for legitimate medical reasons, this ridiculous habit is so pretentious as to be almost comical. Please, barring a room extraordinarily overlit, do not indulge in this phony excess. Perching one's glasses on the top of one's head is only barely more tolerable, simply because it is such a wide-spread practice.

MAKING AN ENTRANCE

Curtsey while you're thinking

what to say. It saves time.

LEWIS CARROLL

Punctuality at a restaurant is even more crucial than at a private dinner party. A restaurant's complex operations are contingent upon the prompt arrival of patrons. A delay of more than ten minutes beyond an appointed reservation requires informing the restaurant immediately.

It is proper ~ and advisable ~ to check a coat,

briefcase, or any commodious item at a cloak-room rather than lug it through a restaurant and eventually turn your table into what appears to be a baggage claim area. I repeat: No gratuitous object belongs on, under, or anywhere near a dining table. This includes eyeglasses, eyeglass cases, cigarette packs, lighters, keys, pens, papers, and bags of any sort. If you bear your host a birthday gift or other tribute, check the gift as well. You can present it as you depart and add your final thanks for the occasion.

If you arrive before the rest of your party, you should feel comfortable waiting at the bar or any other convenient area; if a captain or waiter offers to seat you at the table, by all means ac-cept. Feel free to order a drink while waiting, but plan to pay the tab yourself when the rest of your party arrives.

In restaurants where elegant service is part of the menu, a waiter will automatically carry your glass from the bar to your table when you are being seated. If this is not the case, you may transport your own beverage if you like.

Punctuality is a politeness which a man owes to his stomach.

EMILE GABORIAU

LOCATION, LOCATION, LOCATION

For a host it is entirely correct to make a re-quest for a particular table or area in the dining room, either in advance or upon arrival. If for any tactical reason the maître d' is unable to accede to the request, do make the best of your accommodation unless it is blatantly unsuitable, in which case you have the right to wait for a more acceptable location.

I myself find it easier and more natural to let guests choose their own seats at a restaurant; spontaneous arrangements often produce a more unpredictable and, therefore, a more interesting evening. A host who has planned a specific seating arrangement, only to arrive and find guests already seated at table, would be most gracious to defer to this spontaneity. The alternative is to rearrange guests with humor and good will.

Manners adorn knowledge, and smooth its way through the world.

LORD CHESTERFIELD

MANNERS AND MORES

To some extent correct manners depend on the nature and address of a restaurant. *Not* to vociferously slurp approval of Japanese noodles in Osaka would betray the crudest behavior, while to repeat the ceremony in Paris might stir thoughts of the guillotine. Indigenous customs notwithstanding, there are rules of etiquette that are clearly universal. To be in command of them often requires nothing more than common sense. Perusing a magazine or other reading material at table, for example, is perfectly acceptable at an outdoor café or casual coffee shop, but entirely inappropriate in more luxurious surroundings.

As soon as you are seated, open your napkin and place it on your lap, unless you are dining in a rustic setting, where you can in good faith tuck a napkin around your neck; the same gesture in better restaurants will brand you, at the very least, unsophisticated. If your napkin should slip floorward, you may very well be able to measure a restaurant's professionalism by the promptness with which a waiter retrieves and replaces it. If no one materializes on the spot, ask a waiter for another napkin when he appears.

Similarly, if any piece of silverware should drop, do refrain from snorkeling; rather, ask a waiter for a replacement. And feel free to request the removal of any dispensable item ~ table tents, intrusive candles, ashtrays, or swizzle sticks, for example ~ from the table.

Conversely, do not feel obliged to pick up or extend a plate or glass to help out a waiter unless you are asked to, as such behavior may be perceived as an insult to his professionalism.

I personally do not return food in a restaurant, even if the dish is noticeably overcooked. But it is perfectly acceptable to return food that does not meet any conditions you have specified.

It is also acceptable to ask for additional plates if diners wish to share a dish.

[Etiquette is] a substitute

for war.

ELBERT HUBBARD

HOLD MY CALLS

I am always amazed by displays of narcissistic self-indulgence, and will simply state that headsets should never be seen at a good restaurant. And unless you are a physician on call, beepers and cellular phones are also woefully out of place.

PROPERLY PREPARED CHILDREN

Yes, we have experienced a baby boom. Yes, we are all transfixed by the antics of our own nieces, nephews, sons, and daughters. But, no, as adults we are not obligated to dine with children. Dining with adults is still a privilege children earn. I cannot estimate how many meals are spoiled by fractious, overtired children aching to be home, and their parents are doing no one a favor by permitting such disruptive behavior. In any social situation, children should be prepared to observe and respect the rights of others. If your children are not yet developed or disciplined enough to sit quietly and speak quietly at the table, then do not force them upon others.

And, should it require mentioning, under no circumstances should children be permitted to play with any toys at a dinner table, or sit with personal radios or cassette players strapped to their heads. The rudeness of such unmannerly conduct is so apparent that I am certain polite parents would never dream of permitting it.

PROFESSIONAL COURTESY

Regardless of the level of a restaurant's service, do restrain yourself from treating the staff like indentured servants. Be respectful, never condescending. Do not summon a waiter with a clap of the hand or a wave better suited to flagging a taxi. Employ a subtle nod of the head or attempt to make eye contact. If these gestures are insufficient for receiving attention, voice a soft and modest verbal request: "Excuse me, would you mind . . ." You may certainly shake hands with and address familiar restaurant staff. But if any restaurant personnel should detain you with excessive familiarity, even in an informal setting, you might tolerate a conversation for a courteous moment before turning away, excusing yourself, or quietly stating that such conversation is a distraction.

[Eloquence is] saying the proper thing and stopping.

STANLEY LINK

SEEKING THE
COMFORT ZONE

We have all suffered trendy eateries that seem to revel in bombarding patrons with blinding

91

Music with dinner is an insult both to the cook and the violinist.

G. K. CHESTERTON

lights, pounding music, or shattering echoes refracted off voguishly stark walls. I personally do not shun lively restaurants. In fact, I often dine at the Hard Rock Cafe in New York City because it offers what I consider to be the best club sandwich in the city, and in consequence I prepare myself to endure high-decibel rock and roll anthems as an accompaniment to a tasty meal. Generally I approve of classical music being softly played in a restaurant.

In most restaurants you would be within your rights to request that invasive music or a suffocating thermostat be lowered. But remember that one person's level of comfort may be another's misery: Such a request should be received politely by management, but may not result in the action you hope for. I think it essential that despite any and all discomfort around you, you make a wholehearted attempt to enjoy the occasion as much as possible.

GOOD-NEIGHBOR POLICY

Should you spot a friend or acquaintance while dining, do not interrupt the person's meal or your own party. Considerate behavior dictates a warm but brief nod or wave. I find it presumptuous to expect an acquaintance to shake your hand while he is engrossed in his own repast. If you have a message or desire casual conversation, wait until he is finished eating. Hovering over a table of diners in midmeal is inconsiderate and unfair to both the party and the food.

I do think it is permissible, however, to introduce yourself to someone you want to meet in a restaurant provided you are extremely courteous and wait until the person is not occupied in eating or conversation.

You should not interrupt the conversation of those sitting at a table other than your own. If you are an opera fan and a gentleman or lady seated there hums (ill advisedly, I might add) an aria from an opera that is well known to you and someone at that other table asks the name of the music, do not volunteer an answer. And, for heaven's sake, it is not your business to advise them that it is not good manners to hum at table. Let the maître d' handle the problem for you.

Similarly, if at a neighboring table a waiter mentions the name of a dish ~ not listed on the printed menu, perhaps ~ do not volunteer to explain. If the waiter says, for example, "Tonight we have goujonettes of sole on the menu," and the diner looks puzzled, do not show your superiority by informing him that "A goujon is a small fish found on the sandy bottoms of lakes and rivers in Europe, and is . . ." You will, unconsciously or not, be admitting that you are

Good manners may in

Seven Words be found:

Forget Yourself and think of

Those Around.

ARTHUR GUITERMAN

eavesdropping. You should not have such big ears or such a keen sense of hearing.

WINE WITHOUT WORRY

The wine list is always offered to the host, who should identify himself to the maître d' upon entering the restaurant. However, he may freely seek the counsel of guests before choosing a particular vintage. And he should feel comfortable asking the sommelier or waiter for advice on a good choice.

If wine has been left on the table to breathe, do not assume the magnanimous role of server unless there is no sommelier or waiter to take charge. The sommelier should be available to supervise the pouring of wine throughout the meal. Offer to assist only if you are separated by an obstruction or distance.

In some restaurants wine stewards still offer the opened cork to the host for inspection. While it is pretentious to sniff the cork, it is certainly acceptable ~ and indeed wise ~ to check it to detect a moldy or "corky" smell, which would indicate that the bottle has been improperly stored. Many experts say that when a sample is poured into the host's glass, he ought to merely sniff the aroma as a measure of quality. To my mind a small sip is acceptable. Do save theatrical

Serenely full, the epicure

would say,

"Fate cannot harm me, I

have dined today."

SYDNEY SMITH

swirling in the glass or sloshing in your mouth for your next formal wine tasting. Any wine that smells and tastes vinegary or moldy probably indicates some degree of spoilage. If you are uncertain, defer to the opinion of the sommelier or waiter. In any event, and as a general rule, I suggest you be as certain as possible the wine is unsuitable before refusing the bottle.

On occasion I have tasted a wine and nodded my approval, then when I began drinking I realized it had a "corky" taste. Once you commit yourself to a choice, however, I believe you must swallow it, so to speak. I have seen a very good friend of mine who knows wines send three bottles back before settling on a final choice. I find that beyond the pale.

I have very poor and unhappy brains for drinking; I could wish courtesy would invent some other custom of entertainment.

WILLIAM SHAKESPEARE

You *can* take it with you

I would not hesitate to request leftovers at the end of a casual meal. Many restaurants now wrap extra portions with heavy foil fashioned into fanciful shapes. However, I do think it improper to ask for leftovers in a grand luxe establishment. To my way of thinking the gesture is out of keeping with the surroundings, as well an unintended insult to the chef.

BURNING QUESTIONS

If you are a smoker, you should at the very least save your cigarette until dessert is finished. Even in a so-called smoking section, common courtesy dictates that you ask permission of your table companions before striking a match, since not everyone present may be a smoker.

COMPLIMENTS TO THE CHEF

Sleep not when others speak,

sit not when others stand,

speak not when you should

hold your peace, walk not on

while others stop.

GEORGE WASHINGTON

When a special dinner for a sizable gathering has been prepared, it is perfectly reasonable to request the chef to appear after the meal. Many diners like to express their appreciation in person, and even to discuss the finer points of the menu. An aside to your waiter should suffice to make your wishes known. The host or guest of honor should greet the chef, preferably with a handshake, and introduce her to all other guests at the table. Any further exchange, however delightful, should be brief so the chef can return to his work and the diners to their dinner.

THE MATTER OF MONEY

Financial transactions ought to be clarified in advance. If you intend that several people or

couples should share a dinner check, the intention should be conveyed when planning the occasion. It may be my own insecurity, but I find it
embarrassing when someone says, "Let's split this
check." If I invite people to dinner, the tacit assumption is that I will pay for the evening.

For a dinner-party guest, whether at a neighborhood meeting place or four-star restaurant, it
is only fair and considerate to keep cost in mind
when making menu choices. In many of the
finest restaurants, of course, only the host re-
ceives a menu with prices. Even so, a guest
should demonstrate discretion when making her
selection. She should also avoid "investigating"
the check when it arrives, and should not even
offer to contribute a tip, but simply allow the
transaction to occur without remark, continuing
table conversation. One should extend gratitude
to the host *after* the bill has been paid.

Perusing the check for accuracy is the host's pre-
rogative, although I find the use of calculators at
table tasteless. If you suspect an error, by all means
ask a waiter to double-check his arithmetic.

Courtesy costs nothing.

W. G. BENHAM

TIPPING PERMITTED

Formulas and regulations abound in the matter of tipping, but one rule seems paramount to
me: The amount of a tip should correspond en-

tirely to the degree of one's satisfaction with the meal and service.

According to restaurateurs with whom I have spoken, the average gratuity is fifteen to twenty percent of the total bill (before taxes), which I find wholly appropriate. A slightly larger gratuity may be in order if the food or service has been exceptional. In fine restaurants a fifteen percent tip plus two dollars for each bottle of wine is gracious, regardless of the cost of each bottle. In addition, the general rule when dining in grand luxe restaurants is to tip an attentive wine steward at least two dollars per bottle; this figure should not exceed five dollars even for an outrageously expensive bottle.

If you experience inferior or unacceptable service ~ and I feel only rudeness or total lack of attentiveness qualify ~ you should register a complaint with the restaurant's management. You should not, however, fail to leave a minimum tip for your server. To do so would be to assume that he is responsible for the problem, and this may not be the case ~ inefficiency in the kitchen, for example, might have made proper attention on his part impossible.

If when requesting the check you are informed that you are the guest of the house, it is still proper to leave a tip. Certainly at least twenty percent would be in order. In a luxury establishment you might leave an additional ten to twenty

[Politeness is] an easy virtue, and has great purchasing power.

AMOS BRONSON ALCOTT

dollars for the waiter or captain and twenty dollars for the maître d'. Do remember, however, that extravagant overtipping is invariably seen as an indication of personal insecurity or a gauche display of newfound wealth.

The tip for food service should be left on the check tray; the wine steward's tip may be handed to him discreetly. When larger parties require special attention from the captain, the host should also tip him, at least five dollars. It is also wise to periodically tip a particularly attentive maître d' or captain in a frequented restaurant five dollars. It is acceptable to discreetly palm the tip on entering the restaurant or upon leaving. But never offer a "bribe" to any maître d' in order to procure a table.

Some restaurants now automatically include a fifteen to eighteen percent service charge in the European manner, although you do have the right to adjust that amount according to the level of service you have received.

CHAPTER SIX

THE PARTY'S OVER

One need not plumb the depths of behavioral psychology to learn when to leave a dinner party. Common sense again is one's best guide. When the last course is cleared you will probably adjourn to another setting, perhaps for after-dinner liqueurs. This period following a wonderful meal is a kind of dénouement, but it should be one of relaxed enjoyment. The time for leave-taking should present itself naturally in the course of after-dinner socializing. If you are attuned to its nuances, it is easy to detect a point when interest and attention begin to wane. Often there is a shared sense of nearly sated camaraderie. A simple lull in conversation might signal the right moment to leave. I prefer a high note on which to make an exit ~ a few minutes after I feel the evening has reached its peak of conversation, I depart before the onset of any evident decline.

Guest, withdraw thy foot

from in thy neighbor's house,

lest he be weary of thee, and

hate thee.

PROVERBS 25:17

THE IDEAL MOMENT

Leaving a party too soon or too late constitutes equally poor manners. As I have said, I am always appalled when, two courses into a meal, a guest suddenly makes apologies and rushes off to another engagement. A dinner invitation is almost always assumed to be a request to spend the entire evening. Unless you have clearly made other plans with your hostess, you should forego any other arrangements, or else take a rain check for another evening.

On the other hand, the splendid time you are having may blind you to a hostess's desire to draw the party to a close. Clearly, when she offers no more drink or food, broadly hints about the pleasures of sleep, or goes so far as to start cleaning up, the time is right to exit.

If your guests seem determined to prolong the festivities despite your desire to terminate the evening, as the host you can try for a time to defer to their pleasure with what I like to call consummate Southern charm: unfailing politeness and determination to put their needs first. Of course, a limit exists to gracious tolerance. Once you feel it is simply too late to do even that, you certainly have the right to state, as I do, "I'm very tired. I've had a great time."

Alike he thwarts the
hospitable end
Who drives the free, or stays
the hasty friend:
True friendship's laws are by
this rule expressed,
Welcome the coming, speed
the parting guest.
HOMER

EXIT RIGHT

It is courteous to wait until your host is disengaged from conversation before announcing your intention to leave. Simply express your pleasure in receiving the invitation and your enjoyment of the event. Effusive apologies or explanations for leaving are not necessary. A thank-you ought to be brief and sincere: "I've

had a wonderful time. Let's get together soon."
This is definitely not the time to gossip about the
night's revelations or to commence an engrossing
tête-à-tête.

I think it proper and courteous to acknowl-
edge everyone in the room if possible. The rude
disappearances that punctuate too many fashion-
able Manhattan dinner parties are in fact the height
of narcissism and vulgarity. Good-byes ought to
be as warm as hellos: They deserve the promise
of a closer exchange. However, insincere and in-
gratiating statements—"I'll call you next week
for dinner"—are misleading and uncalled for.

Manners before morals!

OSCAR WILDE

A NOTE OF THANKS

The host of any dinner party deserves, at the
very least, a phone call the next day. After more
formal or special dinners, a thank-you note (on
plain but high-quality stationery) shows great
consideration. A casual note or even a clever
postcard will do nicely for more informal gatherings. In any event, a thank-you should be received no more than one week after the dinner.
It should be simple and express one's genuine appreciation. By all means call attention to and single out one or more factors that particularly
struck you, such as a memorable dish or a lovely
table setting.

I do consider a small gift ~ flowers, a book that you may have discussed ~ a magnanimous gesture after a more formal occasion when the host is a good friend. But I consider the gesture rather gratuitous and patronizing when the host is a new acquaintance. It seems to me to smack of social climbing ~ surely the kiss of death to a budding relationship. I would much rather reciprocate with an invitation of my own to dinner, usually at my home. In such a case, I might call my host before two weeks have elapsed to plan the occasion. If you intend to send a gift, it ought to arrive within a week after the event.

This is undoubtedly a small point, but if you do send a gift after a dinner party, be sure to write your full name on the accompanying note if for any reason your host might confuse you with another guest.

For the most part, the same general rules of leave-taking apply when dining in a restaurant as someone's guest. Never leave before your host "adjourns" the evening, unless by prior arrangement. When you retrieve items from the coat check at the end of the meal, tip the attendant for your own items (one dollar to two dollars is appropriate). And remember that a thank-you call or note is always in order, always elegant, and always appreciated.

[The bore] says a thousand

pleasant things, but never

says, "Adieu."

J. G. SAXE

CHAPTER SEVEN

EATING WELL IS
THE BEST REVENGE

Eating is a sensual experience. No matter how refined we get, we cannot deny two essential facts: Food tastes good, and most of us love to eat. That is why the prospect of eating with our fingers seems so liberating and so much fun. The questions most often asked me about table manners have to do with foods that can be eaten with the fingers: asparagus, artichokes, chicken, spareribs, corn on the cob . . . the list is almost endless.

Along with waste dishes, there are also pieces of flatware that should be placed on the table to assist with eating finger foods ~ a nutcracker for lobster and crab, a snail clamp for snails, and so on.

What follows is a brief list of foods that can be eaten with the fingers and without apology, as well as some suggestions for doing so with the greatest ease and confidence.

Simple pleasures are the last refuge of the complex.

OSCAR WILDE

How to eat

APPETIZERS

Canapés and hors d'oeuvres are the backbone of the cocktail party and are being served increasingly as a first course. As such, they should be easy to eat. At stand-up occasions bite-size tidbits are more manageable than foods that require silverware. If a toothpick is used to spear the food, it should be placed in a receptacle put out for that purpose, in an ashtray, or in one's napkin ~ not back on the serving tray, or in the nearest potted plant. Hot appetizers usually require plates; all appetizers require lots of spare napkins, paper or otherwise.

ARTICHOKES

Whole artichokes should be cooked until tender but not mushy, drained, and arranged neatly in the center of a salad-size plate. Each serving should be accompanied by an individual small bowl with melted butter, the bowl placed on a small saucer. (I like to add a small amount of freshly squeezed lemon juice to the butter.) To eat artichokes, pluck one leaf at a time, starting at the bottom of the vegetable. Put the base of the leaf between your teeth, then extract the tender, fleshy part. You may want to first dip the individual leaf in the melted butter. Place the remainder of the leaves in an orderly fashion on the side of your plate.

Continue until all the leaves are consumed. In the center of the artichoke is an inedible fuzzy portion referred to as the choke. If it has not been removed, cut around the base of it with your salad knife and fork and transfer it to the plate alongside the uneaten leaves. Using the knife and fork, cut the artichoke heart or bottom (they are the same thing) into bite-size pieces, dip in butter, and eat.

[Etiquette is] the noise not

made while eating soup.

ANONYMOUS

Taste is the only morality…

Tell me what you like, and

I'll tell you what you are.

JOHN RUSKIN

ASPARAGUS SPEARS

It is perfectly proper to eat asparagus either with the fingers or with a fork and knife. Hosts should avoid covering the bases of the spears with sauces so they can be picked up with the fingers. They should also try not to overcook them so they do not bend limply when picked up. The spears should be neatly aligned side by side when served. Individual bowls of melted butter for dipping are a nice touch, as are small side plates for any uneaten pieces.

AVOCADOS

Luscious, nutritious avocados with their silky texture are a year-round appetizer staple. Served in dips, they may be eaten with crackers and crudités; sliced, they are eaten with a fork; and when served in halves, they are eaten with a spoon. Avocados discolor rapidly, so try not to prepare them too far in advance. The pit is always removed prior to serving. Empty shells should be left on the plate.

BACON

This is one of those foods that can be eaten with either the fingers or a fork. When bacon strips are served dry and crisp, they are difficult to cut with a fork, so picking them up is perfectly acceptable. Otherwise, a knife and fork, or just a fork, will do.

110

BARBECUED FOODS

These have to be among the sloppiest foods around. Spareribs, hamburgers, charcoal-roasted chicken, grilled corn ~ virtually anything can be grilled today and eaten with the fingers. Have fun, and leave the uneaten elements on the spare plates your hosts have so thoughtfully provided.

BERRIES

Berries are usually eaten with a spoon, as are stewed compotes. Strawberries that are served whole with the hulls left on may be eaten with the fingers holding on to the hull. Leave the hull on the plate afterward.

BOUILLABAISSE

Your guests will need the works for this marvelous dish. Serve hearty portions in deep bowls along with either fish or seafood forks, fish or regular knives, soup spoons, and shellfish crackers or nutcrackers. Don't skimp on the French bread, best served warm. You might want to place a large communal bowl on the table for shells.

[Eating is] the first

enjoyment of life.

LIN YUTANG

CAVIAR

Caviar is probably the most sought-after hors d'oeuvre in the world. In the minds of some purists the ideal way to serve it is without any adornments except buttered toast triangles, the reason being that the taste is so exceptional that it needs no embellishment. If you prefer to offer garnishes, the most common are lemon wedges, finely chopped onions, and chopped hard-cooked egg whites and egg yolks (served separately).

Because caviar is such an extravagant luxury, it tends to bring out the best and worst in diners. Either they are so shy of taking too much that they take too little, or they make voracious pigs of themselves. In order to spare guests difficult decisions, I spoon equal portions of caviar into the center of well-chilled plates. This democratic approach eliminates any anxiety about taking the "right" amount.

Chilled vodka or brut champagne is the classic accompaniment for caviar. Always chill the glasses before serving ~ the refreshing iciness is part of the bang of this fabulous food experience. I always keep a bottle of vodka in the freezer: It does not freeze, and it is alway ready to serve if someone brings a "gift" of caviar.

CHEESES

Always provide a separate knife for each cheese to keep the flavors from mingling. Dessert cheeses ~ delicious accompanied by fruits such as apples, pears, and melons ~ should be eaten with a fork. All cheeses taste better served at room temperature, especially runny ones.

CLAMS AND OYSTERS

There are wonderful china dishes made especially for clams and oysters on the half shell, or they can be served on a regular dinner plate garnished with lemon wedges and accompanied by an oyster fork or a seafood fork. Sauces are served in small individual bowls; extra horseradish or hot sauce can be passed on a condiment tray.

CORN ON THE COB

This is, of course, one of America's finest and favorite vegetables, and for many connoisseurs there is no better way to enjoy corn than straight off the cob. It is best when drained, taken straight to the table, and smeared with butter. You may serve a knife with the corn if the butter is reasonably firm (but not so firm as to prevent easy spreading), slicing the butter and rubbing it neatly up and down the ear of corn that you hold at both ends with your fingers. There are such things as metal corn piercers or handles that can be inserted into the center of the corn cob at each end. I think they are a great waste of time and certainly do not add elegance to this dish. Ideally you should butter a few rows of the corn kernels at a time, eat from one end to the other, then cover another few rows with butter. Of course, the melted butter can be brushed on the corn before it is served, but this takes away part of the pleasure.

[Pleasure is] the only good.

ECCLESIASTES 3:12

If you plan to serve corn at a formal dinner, it should not be served on the cob; rather, the kernels should be scraped from the cob and presented in a more elegant fashion ~ in a light cream sauce, perhaps, or buttered, or sautéed with diced sweet peppers.

DESSERTS

Stewed fruits and compotes are eaten with a spoon; if necessary, the fruit can be held in place with a fork and cut into smaller pieces with a spoon. Moist or messy desserts are perhaps best eaten with both the dessert fork and spoon. Cookies, cream puffs, miniature pastries ~ in other words, bite-size desserts ~ can be picked up and eaten with the fingers. Under no circumstances should a piece of cake or pie be treated in a similar manner.

[Cocktail parties are] midst meatless platters of little treats, the pitiless patter of little feats.

FRANK MALONE

FRIED CHICKEN

The world is divided into people who like to eat chicken with their hands, and those who hate the greasy feeling. There is room for them both. Put out forks and knives along with plenty of napkins. A plate for bones should also be provided.

FROGS' LEGS

These may be eaten with the fingers, but a knife and fork should also be provided. Be sure to put out a spare plate for the inedible parts.

GARNISHES

It is a mystery to me why so many hosts who make otherwise delicious meals ruin the effect at the last minute by using inappropriate garnishes. Harmony is what is wanted, not some bizarre combination like fruit compote with capers, or someting inedible like lemon rind. One of the commonest mistakes is using fresh fruits to garnish warm or hot dishes. Aim for complementary combinations ~ for example, savory foods with nonsweet garnishes like watercress sprigs, chives, delicate lettuces, and bits of truffle. Sweet foods seem to go with fruits in fancy shapes, toasted and pralined nuts, and the like.

If you do not find a garnish appealing, feel free to move it to the side of your plate.

GRAPEFRUIT

Considerate hosts take the work out of eating grapefruit and serve it already sectioned or with the sections loosened if serving grapefruit halves. Remove the seeds before serving. Leave the rind on the plate along with any seeds you may have encountered.

LEMONS

This sunny little citrus fruit is a natural way of waking up and shaking up all sorts of food, from shellfish and vegetables to desserts and beverages. When serving lemons, whether in wedges, slices, quarters, or halves, remove all seeds. Please do not do as many restaurants do and wrap the fruit in cheesecloth or gauze. I think this is a showy conceit when it is just as easy to remove the seeds before serving.

LOBSTER IN THE SHELL

Crack the shells at all points before serving and provide guests with individual shellfish crackers or nutcrackers as well as a seafood fork for extracting the tender meat. In addition, put out at each setting a fish knife or regular knife. A thoughtful extra is a small slender pick that can fit into the smallest claws and feelers.

For a very casual occasion, put out wooden mallets on the table. Garnish each lobster platter with lemon wedges and serve melted butter or a seafood sauce in small individual bowls placed on saucers with spoons.

MELON

Eat with a fork and knife or just a fork when precut, a spoon when served in wedges or halves. Scrape out the pulp and seeds before serving.

NUTS

At a formal dinner, small bowls of shelled nuts may appear on the table; they are usually removed after the salad course. Nut bowls containing unshelled nuts and nutcrackers are very

Good manners are made up

of petty sacrifices.

RALPH WALDO EMERSON

informal, and because of the mess shelling nuts creates they are rarely worth the bother at table. Serve them instead with cocktails and provide receptacles for the shells.

OLIVES, CELERY, PICKLES

The once omnipresent olive, celery, and pickle tray has not entirely disappeared. Guests may serve themselves with the fingers since few hosts today have silver collections that include the venerable pickle fork. Take care when eating olives not to swallow the pits; they should be removed from the mouth with the fingers and placed on the side of one's own plate.

PASTA

Why is it that a food we have been eating since infancy should become intimidating outside the home? If a pasta course, such as linguini, is served with a fork and spoon, it is perfectly acceptable to twirl the pasta in the base of the spoon with the fork. If the pasta is too long to handle comfortably, you can cut it into smaller pieces as needed; there is no need to stuff something that resembles a spool full of BX cable into your mouth. Many other types of pasta can be cut and eaten with a fork.

It is not learning, it is not

virtue, about which

people inquire in society.

It is manners.

WILLIAM MAKEPEACE

THACKERAY

PIZZA

How you eat a wedge of pizza is strictly up to you. If you prefer, cut it into bite-size pieces and eat it with a fork. Most pizza fanciers, however, like to take matters into their own hands, and to my taste this makes perfect sense. It is not a fastidious food and should not be treated as such.

POTATOES

These are a well-loved vegetable and a cross-over finger food. Certainly any meal that offers French fries can be considered informal enough for the fries to be eaten with the fingers. Baked potatoes require some hands-on table preparation on the part of diners: Slit them, slice them, or scoop them out. If you wish to eat the nutritious skins, you can pick them up with your fingers; if not, just leave them on your dish.

SALAD

Why does confusion still exist about how to eat salad? Some people worry that they shouldn't cut the greens with their knives ~ this is silly. There is nothing wrong with cutting up salad into manageable pieces if the leaves or other ingredients seem excessively large. Use your salad fork and salad knife to cut the greens, then rest the knife on the rim of the salad plate. Cut as much as you need for a mouthful at a time, rather than the contents of the entire bowl. It should be

The secret…is never to open

your mouth unless you have

nothing to say.

OSCAR WILDE

said, however, that a considerate host serves greens already broken into manageable bite sizes.

SANDWICHES

This casual fare is most definitely finger food, except in the case of overstuffed sandwiches where the sheer size of the offering requires the assistance of a knife and fork, if not a block and tackle. While Dagwood Bumstead may enjoy such gargantuan repasts, the rest of us might wish for more delicacy.

SHRIMP COCKTAIL

Always be certain to rid the shrimp completely of their shells ~ your goal is not to make work for your guests. Also provide small cups of cocktail sauce for each guest.

SNAILS

These delicacies are best served with snail shell holders, which help secure the shell while two-pronged snail forks remove the meat. You will want to have plenty of French bread for dipping into the shells once the snails are removed. Finger bowls or slightly dampened napkins are invaluable accompaniments.

SOFT-SHELL CRABS

This wonderful springtime delicacy is so tender and sweet that usually the entire crab can be eaten. Since they are always served cleaned, just cut with a knife and fork down the middle and into bite-size sections. The legs can be pulled off and the succulent flesh sucked out. Leave any inedible parts on your plate.

SUSHI

Of all the foreign foods Americans love, sushi is perhaps the one involving the most ritual or, at the very least, little-known rules of etiquette. As with all ritual, the more we understand, the richer the experience becomes.

Basically, sushi is raw fish served on vinegared rice. When it is presented on a "pillow" of pressed rice, with the fish on top, it is considered preferable to pick up the sushi with the fingers. The Japanese dip one end of the sushi into soy sauce, then place the entire piece in the mouth, soy-dipped end first and fish side down so it comes in contact with the tongue. If you feel that the piece is too large or cumbersome, you may bite it in half and return the uneaten portion to the dipping sauce.

If the sushi is rolled in seaweed, it is generally picked up with chopsticks rather than with the fingers. Sashimi, which is simply thinly sliced, boneless fish served without a bed of rice, should also be picked up with chopsticks.

In most Asian cultures, if you are to serve yourself from a communal plate, you should al-

[Etiquette is] the result of that

perfect education in taste and

manner, down to every

gesture.

CHARLES KINGSLEY

ways turn the chopsticks and pick up the food with the large end since the small end has been used for conveying food to your mouth.

WHOLE FRUITS

Apples, pears, kiwis, peaches, and so on may be cut into quarters with a dessert knife and peeled if so desired. Then the fruit may be eaten with the fingers or a dessert fork. If the fruit has a pit or stone, rest it on the underplate.

THE PAPER TRAIL

When you are offered any small items contained in small paper cups ~ such things as petits fours, candied fruits, candy, nuts, hors d'oeuvres, or whatever ~ always remove the item along with the paper container. The empty containers if left in the plate become nothing but clutter. Leave the empty paper cup on your own plate or, if you are standing, dispose of it in a handy refuse receptacle or, perhaps, an ashtray.

[Drinking is] the social

lubricant.

EDWARD STRECKER

HOW TO SERVE

WINE

Wine is so popular today that serving it appears to be the rule rather than the exception. Americans have embraced the grape, and our native soil has produced some of the finest vintages available. Unfortunately, a mystique lingers about wine ~ some people are intimidated about serving it; others worry that they do not know the proper way to drink it. The best advice I can give is simply to relax. Wine is one of man's most inspired creations, and if our forebears knew enough to appreciate it, so should we.

Start with your menu and plan your wine selection around the foods you will serve. Your local wine merchant can help you select the right combinations. Just remember that you want to serve different wines with different courses.

If you plan to serve at least half a bottle per guest, you will not be caught short. Chill white wines and Beaujolais thoroughly, about three to four hours or to 40 to 50 degrees Fahrenheit, before serving. Wines that are fruity and sweet should be chilled to a lower temperature.

Red wines should be poured when their temperature is not less than 65 degrees. It is always best to uncork them to allow them to breathe for an hour before serving. Once opened, they should not be recorked at the table.

Even at home it is customary to sample the wine before serving to determine if it is fit for drinking. The most common problems are corkiness, when wine has taken on the off-taste of the cork, and maderization, when wine tastes moldy because it has been improperly stored.

The difference is, that in the

days of old

Men made the manners;

manners now make men.

LORD BYRON

After a sampling, white wines may be recorked and refrigerated before serving. Of course, red wines may be left uncorked in the dining area.

When pouring wine it is best to hold the bottle firmly around the wine label. To prevent drops of wine from falling down the bottle, gently twist it while pouring. At the table, the bottle of wine should be set directly in front of the host or hostess; for a group of eight or more, a second bottle should be placed at the opposite end of the table and a guest should be designated to pour as needed.

Many people spend too much time worrying over which wineglass to use for specific wines. There is a simple solution to this problem ~ the all-purpose wineglass. With a capacity from nine to twelve ounces, and a shape that cups slightly inward at the rim to capture the wine's aroma, it is fine for any white or red you are serving. Port and sherry are perhaps best served in a glass that holds two to three ounces.

[Conversation is] the only

proper intoxication.

OSCAR WILDE

CHAMPAGNE

Champagne is a true gift from the gods. It is nature's way of saying, "Here's to you, kid," and we love it. So elegant, so exciting, so festive, champagne gives an immediate lift to any occasion. Because it is so beloved, diners tend to drink more of it than other wines, so plan on at least half a bottle for each guest.

123

Champagne need not be served in flat saucer-like glasses; in fact, the taller all-purpose tulip shape classic is preferable, for its slightly rounded rim helps hold in those precious tickly bubbles. Look for glasses with a maximum capacity of three quarters of a cup ~ too oversize and the champagne will get warm, too undersize and what's the point? The tall flute glass may look sophisticated, but because of its small capacity, the host will find himself on constant refill patrol instead of savoring his own glass.

While opening a bottle of champagne may be an exciting ceremony, take care not to point the bottle or cork at any person or object you love. Hold it at a forty-five-degree angle and gently rock the cork back and forth. It is always better to hold on to the cork as you remove it than to have it fly wildly from the bottle, no matter how festive the flight may seem.

Be sure the champagne is thoroughly chilled before serving. Fill your guests' glasses slightly more than half full, and refill accordingly.

A small point to remember is that champagne is a sparkling wine, so it is incorrect to ask a guest, "Would you prefer wine or champagne?" Instead, simply say, "Would you care for a still wine or champagne?" if you are providing your guests with a choice.

When drinking champagne, always hold the glass by its stem. Remember to wait for a signal from your host before taking the first sip ~ he may be planning a toast, and it would look gauche to be caught gulping.

TEA

For elegant occasions you should use a teapot of the most tasteful style your purse can afford. Ideal materials are bone china, porcelain, or earthenware, or you may use a silver teapot that is well polished. The lid on the pot should have a small hole in it, although not so loose that it could fall off when the tea is poured, and should be loosely fitted; the spout should allow for easy pouring. You should always heat the pot before making tea by filling it either with water from a hot water tap or with boiling water from a kettle. When it is very hot, empty the pot and add the loose tea, using one heaping teaspoon for each cup plus "one for the pot." Pour fresh boiling water into the pot and stir. Place the lid on the pot and allow the tea to steep for three to five minutes. When ready, the tea should be poured through a strainer into a cup. It is normally served with sugar and milk. If you or your guests prefer sugar and lemon, the sugar should be added first; it is a minor point, but this will allow the sugar to dissolve more rapidly. If you know the tastes of your guests, you may also offer honey as a sweetener.

The use of silver tea balls (they come in a variety

If we treat people too long with that pretended liking called politeness, we shall find it hard not to like them in the end.

LOGAN PEARSALL SMITH

of sizes and shapes but they are generally round or oval) is acceptable but unnecessary. To use them, the tea balls ~ more properly referred to as tea infusers ~ are opened by a small latch, the tea leaves are added, and the infusers are resealed.

Always serve teacups with a small teaspoon on the side, placed horizontally to the cup's handles. Serve milk in a small pitcher and lemon slices on a small saucer.

As with coffee, it may seem a "precious" thing to do, but it would be best if the cups, as well as the pot, were heated with very hot or boiling water before the tea is poured.

Manners ~ the final and

perfect flower of noble

character.

WILLIAM WINTER

A FINAL WORD ON THE MEANING OF MANNERS

It may seem tedious to repeat a dictum that should be a law of human conduct, but good manners are nothing more than genuine common sense and consideration for others. I do think nearly every rule of social behavior I have detailed may be broken in good faith if one's motives are sincerity and friendship. After all, a dinner party should ultimately be remembered for its company, food, graciousness, and fun, not for its rules of etiquette.

For manners are not idle,

but the fruit

Of loyal nature and of

noble mind

ALFRED, LORD TENNYSON

INDEX